CBT FOR EATING DISORDERS AND BODY DYSMORPHIC DISORDER

CONNOR WHITELEY

No part of this book may be reproduced in any form or by any electronic or mechanical means. Including information storage, and retrieval systems, without written permission from the author except for the use of brief quotations in a book review.

This book is NOT legal, professional, medical, financial or any type of official advice.

Any questions about the book, rights licensing, or to contact the author, please email connorwhiteley@connorwhiteley.net

Copyright © 2024 CONNOR WHITELEY

All rights reserved.

DEDICATION
Thank you to all my readers without you I couldn't do what I love.

INTRODUCTION

Whilst eating disorders are nowhere near the most common mental health condition, they are the deadliest conditions known to us, and treating them is very difficult. Not only because people with eating disorders don't realise the stark and terrifying negative consequences of their condition, but because they don't always want to change.

The same can be said for body dysmorphia where a person has a strong preoccupation with different features of their body that they strongly believe aren't "perfect", leading to some scary behaviours as they try to control and make their features of concern perfect.

So how do psychologists treat eating disorders and body dysmorphia?

Cognitive Behavioural Therapy is the best treatment option we have at this moment in time and it is fascinating to learn about.

What Will This Book Cover?

By the end of this great book, you'll understand these areas of eating disorders:

- What are the different types of eating disorders?
- How common are they and what are their consequences?
- What causes eating disorders?
- How are they treated?

Also, you'll learn the following about body dysmorphia:

- What is body dysmorphia?
- How does body dysmorphia impact a person
- What causes body dysmorphia?
- How is body dysmorphia treated?

There are plenty more great topics to indulge in and learn about in the book.

Who Is This Book For?

Like all of my books, this great book is written for psychology students and professionals wanting to learn more about CBT for Eating Disorders and body dysmorphia. It's okay if you have some knowledge about the topic and you want to learn more or if you know nothing about the topic.

You'll learn a lot in this brilliant, easy-to-understand and engaging book about CBT, how it works and eating disorders.

This is far from a boring, dull textbook. You'll

actually enjoy reading this book.

<u>Who Am I?</u>

Personally, I always love to know who the author is of the nonfiction I read so I know the information is coming from a good source. In case you're like me, I'm Connor Whiteley, the internationally bestselling author of over 40 psychology books.

In addition, I am the host of *The Psychology World Podcast,* a weekly show exploring a new psychology topic each week and delivering the latest psychology news. Available on all major podcast apps and YouTube.

Finally, I am a psychology graduate studying a Clinical Psychology Masters at the University of Kent, England.

So now we know more about each other, let's dive into the great topic of eating disorders, body dysmorphia and CBT.

PART ONE: INTRODUCTION TO EATING DISORDERS

CBT FOR EATING DISORDERS AND BODY DYSMORPHIC DISORDER

INTRODUCTION TO EATING DISORDERS

To kick off this great section of the book on eating disorders, we need to understand first of all what are eating disorders, the different types and most importantly, what makes them different from each other?

That's why in the next two chapters and this first section of the book, we'll be focusing on what are the different types of eating disorders and the different clinical features that make them very different from each other.

Personally, when I first started learning about eating disorders, similar to you I imagine, I didn't think there were any differences. I thought an eating disorder was, well, an eating disorder.

However, as you start reading through the next few chapters, you'll realise there is a lot of fascinating information surrounding eating disorders and why they are so critical to understand.

Also, just to hammer this point home before I discuss the tragic consequences of eating disorders in another chapter. These mental health conditions are some of the deadliest known to us.

Eating disorders kill people and that is why they are so, so important to understand.

<u>What Are The Types of Eating Disorders?</u>

According to the DSM-5 by the American Psychological Association (APA, 2013), there are the following types of eating disorders:

- Anorexia Nervosa (AN)
- Bulimia Nervosa (BN)
- Binge Eating Disorder (BED)
- Avoidant-Restrictive Food Intake Disorder (ARFID)
- Other Specified Feeding or Eating Disorder (OSFED)

For the purposes of this chapter, we'll be focusing on the two eating disorders that are the focus of the book and then in the next chapter I'll introduce you to the other types.

<u>Anorexia Nervosa</u>

Whenever someone mentions eating disorders, I certainly think that anorexia is the most common one that springs to mind for the vast majority of people. I'm no exception and anorexia was the first eating disorder that I really encountered.

However, the problem that I've found in society is that people just use it like it's a meaningless word used to discourage or criticised people. For example, I often hear how someone of a clinically healthy weight is called anorexic by people who don't really know what the words (and deadliness of the condition) means.

So what actually is anorexia?

A person with anorexia has a very low body weight that is below 15% of below what their body weight should be or they have a Body Mass Index (BMI) of 17.5 or less. That is extremely thin and even just writing this paragraph and thinking about how thin that person would have to be is making me very uncomfortable.

In addition, people with anorexia undergo intentional weight loss by avoiding "fattening food" at all costs, they restrict their food intake, they do excessive exercise, conduct self-induced purging behaviour as well as they use appetite suppressants and/or diuretics.

Then this clinical population has a very distorted body image too.

Building upon this, anorexic people have an intense fear of gaining weight or having behaviours that interfere with weight gain. That's why they try to lose as much weight as possible because they are deadly afraid of weight gain.

Interestingly in older versions of the DSM-5, for a woman to be diagnosed with anorexia, they needed to have lost their menstrual cycles and in men, they would have to lose their sexual potency and sexual interest.

Although, if that possible consequence of an eating disorder wasn't scary enough for all readers, then eating disorders can impact development as well. Due to having anorexia can result in puberty being delayed or never happening in the first place (this is called puberty being arrested).

I do find that outcome to be very scary and concerning, because if a person doesn't go through puberty then that will have dramatic consequences for them going forward. They will never be able to have sex, have adult relationships and there are a lot of hormonal and physical changes that occur during puberty that have massive impacts on adulthood.

Let alone the neurological changes that need to happen for the adult brain to form.

<u>Anorexia Diagnostic Criteria</u>

I know it might seem weird us looking at the DSM-5, but for teaching and writing purposes, I find looking at the DSM criteria rather useful in showing you the cluster of symptoms that people with anorexia have, so you can better understand what happens in a person with anorexia.

Therefore, for someone to have a diagnosis of anorexia, they have to show a restriction of energy intake relative to their personal requirements. Resulting in a significantly low body weight for their age, sex, developmental trajectory as well as physical health. Also, you need to know that this "significantly low weight" is defined as a weight that is less than minimally normal or when it comes to children and adolescents, less than that minimally expected.

Secondly, the person would have to have an intense fear of gaining weight or of becoming fat, or show constant behaviour that interferes with weight gain, even though they are already at a significantly low weight.

This is where purging behaviour comes in.

Thirdly, according to the DSM-5, the person needs to have a distorted body image because they have a disturbance in the way they perceive their body weight or shape, they place an unhealthy or too much important on their self-evaluations of their body weight or shape, or they show constant lack of recognition of the seriousness of the current low body weight.

That is another reason why eating disorders are so deadly and hard to treat, because people with these conditions often fail to realise they even have a mental health condition that is causing them serious, serious harm.

Two Types Of Anorexia Nervosa

To wrap up this section, I want to further breakdown two types of anorexia. Firstly, you have Restricted Type Anorexia Nervosa, this is a type of anorexia where the self-starvation isn't associated with purging behaviours that are happening at the same time, like self-inducing vomiting or the inappropriate use of laxatives.

Secondly, you have Binge Eating/Purging Type Anorexia Nervosa, this is a type of eating disorder where the person with the condition regularly engages in purging activities to help control weight gain.

In that sense it is similar to bulimia but bulimia has a lot of its own unique features, that we will look at now.

<u>Bulimia Nervosa</u>

Another type of eating disorder that I admit will feature heavily in the book is Bulimia and this mental health condition is characterised by a person having a fear of gaining weight and they have a distorted body image. Of course that is common with most eating disorders but the main feature of this one is that a person has periods of binge eating followed by periods of fasting or purging behaviours. Both of which are extremely serious and we look at the consequences throughout the book.

In addition, Bulimia normally develops in late adolescence or early adulthood as well as 90% of these cases are women. That is the sad truth of eating disorders, they mainly affect women and to be honest it is a tragedy that anyone regardless of gender develops an eating disorder but women are the most common.

But as you'll see in later chapters, men are important to remember as well when it comes to eating disorders.

Furthermore, if we look at the diagnostic criteria

for Bulimia then a person has to have recurrent episodes of binge eating with one of these episodes being defined by both of the following:

- Eating, in a discrete period of time, like within any two-hour period, an amount of food that's certainly larger than most individuals would eat in a similar period of time under similar circumstances.
- A sense of lack of control over their eating during the episode. For instance, the person believes they can't stop eating or even control what or how much they're eating.

Another criterion a person has to meet is they have to have recurrent inappropriate compensatory (purging) behaviours that prevents them gaining weight. This can include excessive exercise, fasting, self-induced vomiting, misuse of laxatives, diuretics, or other medications.

The idea of self-induced vomiting is definitely something that springs to mind whenever I think about bulimia, and it is these purging behaviours that are important to a person's faulty and biased psychological processes.

In addition, the diagnostic criteria states that this binge eating and inappropriate compensatory behaviours must both occur at least once a week for 3 months on average.

Now of course we can debate clinical cut-offs and how we might be putting people at risk that have the condition but haven't been showing the symptoms for 3 months yet, but this is an interesting area for discussion, and I will admit that 3 months compared to other mental health conditions is very, very short. That's a good thing considering how deadly eating disorders are.

Finally, people with bulimia have to show that their self-evaluation is heavily and unjustifiably influenced by their body shape as well as weight. Also, bulimia can explain why a person doesn't meet a diagnosis of anorexia nervosa, because as you know from the section above, these conditions involve different features.

Overall, now that we're starting to understand what are eating disorders, let's explore some more. As well as even though the DSM is heavily flawed and clinical psychology is in dire need of a good replacement, looking at the cluster of symptoms can be useful for teaching purposes as it helps to introduce you to what each mental health condition involves.

Let's see what other eating disorders exist.

MORE ON TYPES OF EATING DISORDERS

Continuing with our introduction to the different types of eating disorders, in this chapter, we're going to look at some really interesting conditions. Granted, we don't focus on them very much in the rest of the book. Yet they are still good to learn about some will equally interest and horrified you.

Also, in case anyone was interested in any potential differences between the American DSM and World Health Organisation ICD-11 when it came to eating disorders, there aren't that many differences which is why we don't talk about them.

However, the major types of eating disorders according to ICD-11 are as follows:

- Anorexia Nervosa
- Bulimia Nervosa
- Binge Eating Disorder
- Avoidant- Restrictive Food Intake Disorder

- Other Specified Feeding Or Eating Disorders
- Feeding Or Eating Disorders Unspecified

<u>Binge-Eating Disorder (BED)</u>

Maybe this type of eating disorder has one of the most friendly anacronyms within all of psychology, because who doesn't like a nice bed?

However, don't let that fool you because BED is a very serious condition like all eating disorders. Due to this eating disorder is characterized by recurrent episodes of binge eating similar to Bulimia but unlike that condition, Bed doesn't involve fasting or purging behaviours.

As a result, these people tend to be overweight and have a long history of failed dieting and weight-loss attempts with the condition normally developing in late adolescence or early adulthood.

Interestingly, I would like to know how many of the people on TV programmes, like My 600 Pound Life, have these conditions. There's no way to tell because these programmes don't even begin to investigate these mental health or psychological aspects in much depth, because they only focus on the medical aspects.

But given what we talk about in this brief section on the condition, I actually wouldn't be surprised if these people did meet a good number of the criteria below.

Anyway, if we look at the diagnostic criteria from the DSM-5 then like bulimia, a person has to have recurrent episodes of binge eating with one of these episodes being defined by both of the following:

- Eating, in a discrete period of time, like within any two-hour period, an amount of food that's certainly larger than most individuals would eat in a similar period of time under similar circumstances.
- A sense of lack of control over their eating during the episode. For instance, the person believes they can't stop eating or even control what or how much they're eating.

However, unlike bulimia, there are extra reasons and boxes to tick in response to the binge-eating. Since criterion B of the condition requires people to have binge-eating episodes that are associated with three (or more) of the following features:

- Eating alone because of feeling embarrassed by how much they're eating.
- Eating until feeling uncomfortably full.
- Eating large amounts of food when not feeling physically hungry.
- Eating much more rapidly than normal.
- Feeling disgusted with themselves, depressed, or feeling very guilty afterwards.

Whilst there are other smaller pieces of diagnostic criteria to meet that's all I want to cover in this chapter because this isn't a condition we'll focus on in the book, and the Criterion so far shows you how this condition is similar to bulimia just without the deadly purging behaviours.

<u>ARFID (Avoidant Restrictive Food Intake Disorder)</u>

For our penultimate eating disorder, we need to look at ARFID, this is when a person has an eating or feeding disturbance, like an apparent lack of interesting in or eating, and this can be for some interesting reasons.

Sometimes people with ARFID aren't interested in food or eating because they avoid it based on sensory characteristics. One interesting thing about these sensory characteristics is when I was researching this book, I found a lot of comments from parents from autistic children back in the dark days of the COVID-19 pandemic were extremely stressed out because they couldn't get pasta.

And pasta is a very good food for autistic children from what I've heard, because it doesn't have the sensory difficulties that other foods have. Then because this pasta wasn't available, parents were extremely stressed that their child wasn't going to eat anything.

I cannot even begin to imagine how awful that must have been for them.

Also, for other people their avoidance behaviours is based on a concern about the aversive consequences of eating. That's why psychological support and Cognitive Behavioural Therapy can be needed.

Moreover, if a person has a constant failure to meet their nutritional and energy needs then this leads to significant weight loss, and in children this means they cannot gain weight, they experience a significant nutritional deficiency, they become dependent on enteral (tube) feeding and a stark interference with their psychosocial functioning.

For instance, one of my favourite chapters in my Developmental Psychology book is the poverty chapter, because there are some great studies out on how lack of food and nourishment leads to brain deficits that continue the cycle of poverty.

However, for someone to have ARFID, the lack of eating cannot be explained by a lack of good or culturally sanctioned practices. For instance, you cannot say that a Muslim person has ARFID during ranadan because the lack of interest in food and eating during daylight hours is a culturally sanctioned practice, and there are a ton of rules allowing people to eat if needed.

Moreover, ARFID doesn't only happen in people with Anorexia or bulimia, because there isn't a disturbance in the way a person perceives their body weight or shape. There is only a lack of interest in eating and food.

Yet if this does happen in the context or "inside" a medical condition or a mental health condition then this absolutely warrants independent clinical attention, because you need to know if someone has ARFID because not only does this need treating alongside the other condition, but this would have massive treatment implications. You cannot get "better" if you don't have the nourishment or energy to heal or do therapy.

Finally, there are three main subtypes of ARFID. Firstly, you have people that don't eat enough or show little interest in feeding. Secondly, you have people who only accept a limited diet because they don't like the food's sensory features. Thirdly, you have people with ARFID that refuse to eat because they hate the eating experience.

Other Specified Feeding Or Eating Disorder (OSFED)

Moving onto another of the lesser well-known types of eating disorders, OSFED is one that I had never even heard of before I really started to research this topic. Therefore, this eating or feeding disorder is a condition that causes a person significant clinical distress and/ or impairment in different areas of their life, but the person doesn't meet the diagnostic criteria for another feeding or eating disorder.

In other words, this is sort of a miscellaneous category.

In addition, there are a few different named eating disorders that are classed as OSFED. For example, Atypical Anorexia Nervosa is a very interesting one because this is a type of anorexia where a person meets every single criteria for anorexia except the weight condition, because they aren't underweight to the extent that anorexia requires.

In addition, Subthreshold Bulimia Nervosa is another OSFED condition because this is where a person meets the criteria for bulimia but not the requirement surrounding the frequency of the purging and binge-eating episodes.

Penultimately, you can have Subthreshold Binge Eating Disorder where a person meets all the criteria for BED but this condition occurs at a lower frequency.

Finally, you can have purging disorder where a person shows purging behaviour without the binge-eating episodes. As well as Night Eating Syndrome where a person shows excessive nighttime eating behaviours.

Overall, I have to admit that this is a good example about why clinical cut-offs aren't the best, because like Subthreshold Binge Eating Disorder, the person clearly has BED but not to the severity that mental health services are willing to act. Therefore, you might be able to argue that if this person gets treated now then they will never have to go to mental health services because they would have been supported earlier, that would save the services money, but then who would deliver this preventive care?

It is always a hard one and these OFSED conditions are interesting, I have to admit.

Yet I haven't mentioned yet, how common are these eating disorders and what other basic information should you know about them?

PREVALENCE, COMORBIDITY AND CULTURAL AND SOCIAL FACTORS FOR EATING DISORDERS

Now we understand what are the different types of eating disorders, we now need to understand the prevalence rates (how common they are), what mental health conditions that tend to develop alongside eating disorders and how social as well as cultural factors influence the development and maintenance of eating disorders.

This is a very interesting chapter I promise.

Unfortunately, if we turn our attention towards Anorexia Nervosa for now, this is the deadliest mental health condition known to us due to it has the highest mortality rate of all mental health conditions, and it doesn't just kill a person outright.

Since 54% of Anorexia deaths are secondary deaths because of complications of the Anorexia Nervosa. Then 5-10% of all deaths in Anorexia are because of cardiac complications that the Anorexia causes and 27% of the deaths are suicides.

Personally, I think that single paragraph explains why this book is so important, because yes, all of us current or future psychotherapists learn about depression, anxiety and the other really common mental health conditions. And I will not lie if depression goes untreated then suicide is a very real possibility.

But with eating disorders and body dysmorphia, death is very, very likely and as therapists, it is our job to try to stop that. We might not always succeed but if I know because of my past difficulties, I could never treat or work with people with eating disorders. Yet even if I could get a single person interested in this fascinating area then I might have done my job as an author.

And that single person might go on to become a therapist, work with clients with eating disorders and hopefully change some lives for the better across their career.

Maybe save a few lives too.

Furthermore, I won't lie here and say that the impacts and effects of Anorexia aren't heart-breaking because some of the following consequences of Anorexia on the body are a little heart-wrecking:

- Tiredness
- Dry skin and brittle hair
- Cardiac arrhythmias (abnormal heart rhythm)

- Low blood pressure
- Slow heartbeats
- Kidney and gastrointestinal problems
- The absence of menstrual cycles (amenorrhea)
- The development of lanugo, a soft, downy hair, on the body
- Hypothermia, often making a client feel cold even in hot environments.

Almost all of these factors are down to the anorexia and lack of eating making a client malnourished and starve. That's why the body tries to keep itself alive by maladaptively changing itself, because the body can't see the point in "wasting" energy and nutrients on the lining of the womb and a period, because it would rather save those nutrients and keep the client alive a little longer.

The body's job is to survive, which is another reason why mental health conditions are so fascinating to me.

Overall, when it comes to Anorexia, only 46% of clients experience a full recovery after therapy, another 33% only experience partial recovery and 20% of all clients don't recover at all. That's why research into new therapies is always needed.

In addition, when a client has Anorexia, there is a chance they will have what's known as a comorbid condition, so they will have another mental health condition too. I explain why this makes treatment more challenging in later chapters.

Therefore, these conditions are common to have alongside Anorexia:

- Depression
- Emerging borderline personality disorder
- Anxiety and obsessionality
- Autism spectrum Conditions
- Substance abuse
- Chronic fatigue syndrome

Another difficulty about a client having Anorexia and another condition on top of that is the other condition can intensify the eating disorders symptoms and have a big impact on treatment. For instance, decreasing the chance of recovery and increasing the likelihood of them dropping out. That's why treatment always needs to address these co-existing conditions and eating disorders.

Finally, to wrap up our look at Anorexia, the average age of onset for the condition is between 15 and 19 years old, and it is the most common cause of weight loss in teenage girls and inpatient admissions, with 90% of this clinical population being females. Due to the lifetime prevalence rates for females is 0.5% but this might be higher or lower across cultures and time.

The causes and social and cultural factors we look at in the next few chapters.

Prevalence Rates of Bulimia

If we turn our attention towards Bulimia, this is unfortunately higher than anorexia because the lifetime prevalence is 1-3% among females and for males the prevalence rates is 0.1-0.3%.

Yet the news gets worse because the incidence rate of bulimia in women in Western cultures appears to be increasing (Keel & Klump, 2003) as well as the condition is highly comorbid with a range of other mental health conditions. For example, personality disorders (now called Complex Emotional Needs), major depression, substance abuse and dependency,

Prevalence Rates of Binge-Eating Disorder

As you can guess when it comes to BED, there is an overlap between this condition and Bulimia but the lifetime prevalence in the general population of BED is 3% but it can be as high as 30% in people looking for weight loss treatment (Dingemans et al., 2002).

That is scary.

Also, whilst the majority of this clinical population is female, the incidence rate in females is only 1.5 times higher than in men (Stice et al., 2000) so there might not be as high of a difference between the sexes as you think. As well as BED is triggered by dieting, stress, negative body image and boredom.

Cultural And Demographic Differences In Eating Disorders

This next section I think is really interesting and it definitely gives you some food for thought, because

I really enjoy learning about how social norms and cultural factors impact our behaviours. Therefore, in bulimia, people are a lot LESS likely to develop the condition if they haven't been exposed to western ideals (Keel & Klump, 2003).

Furthermore, African American women were less likely to have eating disorders than American white women (Lovejoy, 2001), but sadly in the USA, rates of eating disorders in Asian immigrants are increasing (Chamorro & Flores-Ortiz, 2000).

Similarly, when it comes to anorexia, people are a lot LESS likely to develop the condition if they haven't been exposed to western ideals (Keel & Klump, 2003).

Overall, females are ten times more likely to develop eating disorders than male and one reason for this is because female thinness could be viewed as an important social value (Spitzer et al., 1999). Yet we'll be looking at different social and cultural factors impacting eating disorders later on.

As well as eating disorders are higher in groups where their body weight and shape are of more importance to them. Like ballet dancers and athletes.

Leading us onto our next chapter of what causes eating disorders?

WHAT CAUSES EATING DISORDERS?

After understanding what eating disorders are, some basic information about them and the different types of this range of mental health conditions, now we need to understand what causes them to develop and become maintained in the first place.

Since a lot of people presume that once a mental health condition develops it is always there and it takes root immediately, I completely understand why they think that (I used to think that as well) but for a mental health condition to become serious enough to get a diagnosis. It has to be maintained for some reason.

There has to be a reason why people keep those maladaptive behaviours and coping mechanisms.

That's why in this chapter, we'll be learning about the biological and some of the sociocultural influences. Then in the next few chapters, you'll learn about how peer influences, familial factors, experiential factors and psychological and dispositional factors lead to the development and maintaining of eating disorders.

Biological Factors

Like all behaviour, eating disorders are a product of the interaction between biological, psychological and social factors. Therefore, in terms of biological factors, a person's genetics do play a role, because the heritability of eating disorders could be higher than 50% (Klump et al., 2001) and this is supported by the fact that eating disorders tend to run in families.

Also, there is significant co-impact of unique environmental factors, more on those factors later on, but it must be noted that different genes and different genetic factors are involved in bulimia and anorexia.

Although, there are non-genetic factors playing a role in eating disorders because feeding behaviour and the disordered eating is reinforced by endogenous opioids and serotonin metabolites. Therefore, it has been argued that there is a neuroendocrine dysfunction in eating disorders.

Then again, if this is true then this biological theory still fails to explain the psychological thoughts and factors behind eating disorders, as well as the social factors that we will look at now.

Social Media

To introduce social media to everyone, we all

know that social media is increasing each year, especially in young people, and this could cause a young person to form an "over-association" between self-worth and body image. For example, if I get slimmer and slimmer for my Instagram photos then I will get more likes, and more likes makes me feel good.

These social media posts reinforce and only encourage body comparison and cognitive distortions (Sidani et al., 2016) to develop, and this will be explored more in the next chapter.

Media

Building upon this, there are increases in eating disorders associated with the changes in how the media represents the so-called ideal female body shape. Since when there is a gap between the ideal body shape and what the person looks like, this can increase body shape dissatisfaction.

And high levels of body shape dissatisfaction is associated with watching TV programmes that present idealized female images (Tiggerman & Pickering, 1996). Leading to people shifting to a low-calorie food trend and making a stronger value judgment of obesity versus thinness.

In other words, people value thinness over obesity higher and higher regardless of the extremes and damaging behaviours they do to reach these goals.

Body Shape Dissatisfaction

To finish off this introduction to the causes

behind eating disorders, body shape dissatisfaction is important and this is defined as "the gap between a person's actual and ideal weight and shape".

This is a critical concept in eating disorders because most theories do rightly blame body dissatisfaction for the development and maintenance of the condition. Since body dissatisfaction is likely to trigger dieting behaviour (Stice, 2001).

However, just because someone has high levels of body dissatisfaction doesn't mean they automatically have or do go on to develop an eating disorder.

Leading us to wonder what factors and influences are needed for eating disorders to occur. This we will explore in the next few chapters.

WHAT'S WRONG WITH HAVING THE PERFECT BODY?

Of all the podcast episodes, I've ever done on The Psychology World Podcast, I have to admit that the article below just might be my favourite ones ever. It is very important to eating disorders because this article looks at body image ideals and it helps to explain a lot of the factors causing eating disorders in more depth.

This is a critical chapter to understand and read and I loved this one, so I know you will too.

Enjoy!

<u>What's Wrong With Having The Perfect Body?</u>

Body image concerns and the negative impact on both women's and men's mental health make for concerning reading and its effects are both deadly and extremely dangerous. I looked at this topic before in *Body Negativity In Boys And Why This Is A Silent Crisis*, but in today's episode we need to look at what's wrong with having the perfect body? And more importantly, what's driving this obsession with the perfect body and more. This is a great psychology podcast episode for anyone interested in clinical psychology, eating disorders and male mental health.

What's Wrong With Having The Perfect Body?

The idea of the perfect body is something that really does influence society and you could even argue that it plagues us because it is everywhere. It is on social media, in movies and TV programmes. Since if you think about the last major film or television programme you watched that was a blockbuster then you probably imagine scarily thin and sexy women with perfect beautiful bodies with long perfect hair. Or men with stunning muscles, the perfect body and the perfectly strong jawline and more.

Of course, none of these definitions are healthy, natural or positive in the slightest and there have been changes in recent years.

Since in recent years, the bodies of these actors and actresses are becoming more and more extreme and further away from the average body of the average man or woman. For example, if you look at Hugh Jackman in the early 2000s his body was described as being perfect in those days but now he has become more increasingly lean and massive over these two decades, with Jackman saying that the next wolverine is going to be even bigger and the biggest ever wolverine.

This is also supported by a recent accountability

post that actor Jake Stormeon posted on his personal Instagram account saying that in his 20s when he was filming The Outpost his job required him to be shirtless most of, if not all the time, and that required him to do a hell of a lot of things for his body. And as a fan I can confirm there is a difference but as an average man, I think it is a healthy difference.

Now I am not singling with him out but his honesty makes a good point. He didn't say he wanted to do these extreme things to his body, he said his job required it.

Again this basically harks back to the idea of the perfect body image and what film companies require.

<u>Body Image and Social Media</u>

In addition, social media reflects this increase in impossible standards for the so-called perfect body and as an Instagram user I know that Instagram is literally clogged with tons of "thirst trap" selfies featuring muscular men with minimal body fat percentage. As well as Longergan et al. (2021) found that posts like these receive a disportionatetly positive response from other social media users, so this reinforces the men who post this way.

In other words, this positive response reinforces these impossible standards and the so-called need for these standards in the people who look like this.

Moreover, in 2020 a quantitative study by Gultzow et al. analysed photos posted by men on Instagram and found the exact same thing. Most photos posted in the sample that depicted a lot of muscles and lean body mass. Then to measure this perceived need for males to be muscular, McCreary created a psychometric scale measuring "drive for muscularity" in 2017, and the researcher noted that the no-body-fat physique, packed with muscles is often "considered the male ideal".

Also McCreary (2017) found that men felt worse about their physical appearance after looking at and absorbing the idealised and hyper-muscular images and other content found on Instagram. As well as Carfi et al. (2002) showed these body image concerns reduce a man's confidence, self-esteem and overall life satisfaction just like they do for women.

Why Am I Not "Picking" On Instagram Here?

I just wanted to make it clear to people here on the website and on the podcast that I am not picking on Instagram here but I do want to highlight it. This is where the research is done, Instagram is an image-based platform so it is perfect for sharing idealised body images and their recommendation algorithms are scary. I will admit on this podcast because I believe in honesty and telling you the truth and on Instagram I clicked on an image of these idealised bodies once or twice and the next time I went onto Instagram my recommendation feed was filled with them.

And I mean filled.

Therefore, these social platforms of course play a major role in pushing this harmful content which is understandable considering the positive reaction they get.

<u>Male Body Image and Wider Society</u>

If we step back from social media for a moment then we can see that this is also reflected in general, wider society since Luicano (2007) found that American men grow up believing that muscles signal masculinity. In other words, having muscles makes you a man and all that absolute rubbish.

Therefore, these distorted expectations do more than just contribute to the constant creation and sharing of shirtless photos on social media. These beliefs and attitudes can warp into the body image disorder known as muscle dysmorphia. This is a dangerous condition when a sufferer becomes convinced that their body is too skinny, weak and small.

And this problem is only getting worse.

As a result of a 2019 study of 700 American men between the ages of 18 and 24 showed that more than 20% of men had a disordered relationship to food because of their desire to get bigger and more muscle-bound. These young men were eating too much due to "bulking up" requires a high-calorie intake, they put their own health at risk by using anabolic steroids or they took dietary supplements like extra protein.

<u>International Body Image Concerns</u>

Sadly these body image concerns are not contained to only the USA because this is an international crisis since whilst up to 40% of

American men do feel anxious about their weight according to Frederick et al. (2022). In the UK according to the Mental Health Foundation, more than 20% of English men admit they try to dress in a way that conceals parts of their body in 2019.

In addition, 11% of English men reported suicidal thoughts because of their negative body image concerns as well as 4% said they had already tried to hurt themselves for this exact reason.

Then in France, the Journal of Men's Health (2014), up to 85% of French men reported they weren't happy with their bodies because they thought they didn't have enough muscles.

Finally for this section, this was all only made worse by the COVID-19 pandemic because the health-related anxieties that were swimming around in society could have made these body image issues worse. A 2021 study supported by this by finding social distancing was linked with higher male dissatisfaction with their muscles and weight.

Overall, before we move on, I will just say this. These body image concerns, they kill people, they harm people and they can twist someone's mind in horrific ways. I already mentioned in the last podcast episode on this topic that eating disorders (that these concerns can lead to) kill people and are some of the deadliest mental health conditions in the world.

So I don't say this to scare you at all. I say this because enough is enough and we need to help fix this international mental health crisis.

Why Don't Men Talk About Their Body Image Concerns?

As Rasisanen and Hunt pointed out in a 2014 article for the BMJ Open Journal, a lot of men just don't want to talk about these issues with their friends and family members. They feel insufficient enough already in their own heads without adding to the concerns about their family and friends judging them or even agreeing with them (I highly doubt they would but these are the sort of things people with body image issues tell themselves). Therefore, these men stay silent out of fear of expressing these feelings and risking them being seen as even less manly.

This is why I personally hate the idea of "manliness" because it is pathetic. I am sorry but I have no time for people who parade around the idea of manliness because they are doing so much damage to society, the mental health of innocent people and more that I just don't want to hear from them.

I do have time for the victims of the "manliness" culture and people that want to help people, and this is why I do these podcast episodes. I want to help people and I want people to realise that the traditional ideas of "manliness" aren't only damaging but very outdated.

Furthermore, as the 2014 article pointed out, even if these amazing men who are perfect in their own way get enough courage to ask for help. Some are dismissed because people believe body image issues are only for women and men don't have them.

This is why knowing how to identify what to look for in men with body image issues is critical.

How To Know If A Man Has Body Image Issues?

Very quickly for the last section of the episode, if you think that a friend or family member is having body image issues then maybe look out for these signs. This isn't official advice but this could be a starting point if you're worried.

Maybe your family member or friend has gained a lot of weight all of a sudden, maybe they've been talking about their body a lot lately or they could be bulking up excessively. Or maybe they have been spending a lot more time in the gym or in front of a mirror lately.

This could show that a body-image issue is present.

If this is the case then maybe they should check out a therapist specialising in eating disorders. Then they will help the client (if they want the help) to change their obsessive thoughts about their physical appearance and reorient them to focus less on their exterior benefit and more on the effects of their long-term well-being.

Clinical Psychology and Eating Disorders Conclusion

I know in the last podcast episode I spoke about my own eating and body image issues in the past and that is why I love talking about this topic. I will not pretend that I have had these issues so dire that it has destroyed me but it honestly could have. I could have had an eating disorder and hospitalised a few years ago because I hated my body that much.

That is why I make sure I make three meals a day even if I am NOT hungry.

So to end this episode, I want to remind you that body image issues will be seriously harmful to people in the end and they are no joke. If you're a man or woman with a body image issue then please talk to someone, get their opinion on it and if you need it then please seek professional help.

Please don't suffer in silence because you are perfect just the way you are and there is a massive difference between wanting to be healthy. And wanting to have the perfect body.

Having the perfect body never ends well.

Clinical Psychology References

Barlett, C. P., Vowels, C. L. & Saucier, D. A. (2008). Meta-analyses of the effects of media images on men's body-image concerns. Journal of Social and Clinical Psychology 27(3).

Cafri, G., Strauss J. & Thompson, J. K. (2002). Male body image: Satisfaction and its relationship to well-being using the somatomorphic matrix. International Journal of Men's Health; 1 (2)

Frederick, D. A., Crerand, C. E., Brown, T. A., Perez, M., Best, C. R., Cook-Cottone, C. P., Compte, E. J., Convertino, L., Gordon, A. R., Malcarne, V. L.,

Nagata, J. M., Parent, M. C., Pennesi, J., Pila, E., Rodgers, R. F., Schaefer, L. M., Thompson, J. K., Tylka, T. L., & Murray, S. B. (2022). Demographic predictors of body image satisfaction: The U.S. Body Project I, Body Image, Volume 41, 17-31.

Gültzow, T., Guidry, J. P. D., Schneider, F. & Hoving, C. (2020). Male body image portrayals on Instagram. Cyberpsychology, Behavior, and Social Networking. 23(5), 281-289.

Lonergan, A.R., Mitchison, D., Bussey, K. & Fardouly, J. (2021). Social Media and Eating and Body Image Concerns Among Men and Boys. In J. M. Nagata, T. A. Brown, S. B. Murray & J. M. Lavender (Ed.), *Eating disorders in boys and men*, pp/ 307-316. Cham, Switzerland: Springer.

Luciano, L. (2007). Muscularity and Masculinity in the United States: A Historical Overview. In J. K. Thompson & G. Cafri (Eds.), *The muscular ideal: Psychological, social, and medical perspectives* (pp. 41–65). American Psychological Association. https://doi.org/10.1037/11581-002

McCreary, D. R. (2007). The Drive for Muscularity Scale: Description, Psychometrics, and Research Findings. In J. K. Thompson & G. Cafri (Eds.), *The muscular ideal: Psychological, social, and medical perspectives* (pp. 87–106). American Psychological Association. https://doi.org/10.1037/11581-004

The Mental Health Foundation. (2019, Nov 12). Millions of men in the UK affected by body image issues – Mental Health Foundation survey. Retrieved from https://www.mentalhealth.org.uk/about-us/news/millions-men-uk-affected-body-image-issues-mental-health-foundation-survey

Räisänen, U. & Hunt, K. (2014). The role of gendered constructions of eating disorders in delayed help-seeking in men: a qualitative interview study. Retrieved from https://bmjopen.bmj.com/content/bmjopen/4/4/e004342.full.pdf

Swami, V., Horne, G. & Furnham, A. (2021, Feb 15). COVID-19-related stress and anxiety are associated with negative body image in adults from the United Kingdom. Personality and Individual Differences, 170.

Valls, M., Bonvin, P., & Chabrol, H. (2014). Association between muscularity dissatisfaction and body dissatisfaction among normal-weight French men. Journal of Men's Health, 10(4), 139-145.

BODY NEGATIVITY IN BOYS AND WHY THIS IS A SILENT PROBLEM

Whilst this was the article I wrote for my first-ever podcast episode on eating disorders, I wanted to focus on the last chapter first of all because that chapter discussed more about body ideals and the damaging impact of the media.

However, this is a really good chapter because a lot of what we discussed earlier on in the book and in the other places focus on the struggles that girls have, and whilst girls and women are the majority of the eating disorder population, men and boys cannot be left behind too.

Therefore, this is a very useful introduction and guide to eating disorders in boys and most importantly, why this is a silent problem.

Enjoy.

***

Body Negativity In Boys and Why This Is A Silent Problem?

Whenever we think about teenagers with body image and body positivity problems, we always think that girls are the main people that suffer with these problems. We believe that girls are always the people with body negativity, and that boys are very safe from this problem. But a lot of recent research suggests that the majority of boys have massive body image problems, so why do we still focus on girls when there is clearly a much larger problem? That's what we'll explore in today's podcast episode.

Body Negativity In Boys

One of the miniature themes of this podcast is that I always like to investigate underexplored areas and help to bring them to the attention of all of us. For example, that's why I investigate suicide on the podcast, how mental health conditions could in fact be adaptions and not *disorders* amongst other topics. Therefore, I really want to highlight how boys can be very badly affected by body image issues, and how this is not a problem limited to girls.

In addition, the author of the book *Being You: The Body Image Book for Boys* mentioned that young men and boys are often at a complete loss when it comes to talking about their body image concerns, even if these concerns start early in life.

And before I start talking about studies and the

research side of this argument, I want to give you a little bit of my own personal interest in the topic area. Since as a child I was obese and as you imagine I was an easy target for bullies so I was really bullied for it for years and years. As well as even though I was basically change between being underweight and having a normal weight depending on the week and my body attitude, I still think I will always see myself as fat.

Wow, even writing that's difficult because during my first year of university, several people did suspect I had developed an eating disorder because I was barely eating maybe a thousand calories a day and I was doing extreme amounts of exercise. Looking back I know that wasn't healthy and I was had that I didn't hospitalise myself, but it just does to show how powerful bullying can be, and whilst there are other factors that are more or less influential for other people. That's my story in short.

In addition, McLean et al. (2018) found that even boys that are as young as 6 years old believe that muscles make boys look better, and one of the real dangers about this particular belief is that before puberty, boys aren't apt to build anything looking like the bulky muscles of bodybuilders. Resulting in a lot of young boys being disappointed in their bodies from an early age.

Personally, I think that's heart-breaking and a massive shame that somewhere in our society, we have created an atmosphere where pre-teenagers feel the need to get muscles to look good.

And possibly connecting to my own personal story, this concern about body image isn't just a superficial concern as it can and does have very serious consequences. Like eating disorders because one-fourth to one-third of eating disorder patients are male, as well as eating disorders are among the deadliest mental health conditions. If you want to see the source for that fact see the reference list below for the website.

So yes, it is very, very fair to say that body image issues can kill people.

Finally for this section, a very concerning finding is that this problem isn't going away since a growing number of boys, as much as an 11% growth (Glazer et al., 2021), are using steroids or supplements to increase their muscle mass. As well as TikTok seems to only encourage these maladaptive body image behaviours by increasing the popularity of trends like "dry scooping" protein powder. This is where you take a pre-workout consumption of chalky powders without dissolving them in water first.

That is actually very dangerous.

Why Don't We Talk About Body Image Issues in Boys?

Now this is one of my favourite areas to explore because I really am interested in why certain mental health conditions are steered or limited towards only affecting certain populations or genders, or at least that's what the mainstream wants us to believe.

Thankfully, unlike other areas of mental health, like telling female rape survivors in the last century that what they experienced didn't matter, the body image conversation around boys isn't quite as dark, but it is still outrageous.

Since the reason why body image and negativity surrounds girls and women so much is because out of concerns over the decades' long marketing and objectifying and basically society telling women they had to be thin, attractive and feminine if they wanted to have any hope of succeeding in society. Well that's the gist.

Therefore, to combat the damage this marketing and other societal-level factors had done over the decades, the focus on was protecting the mental health of women and young girls. However, this has caused men and boys to have a lot of trouble speaking out about their own mental health in general but especially surrounding their body image.

Furthermore, in the book, *Being You: The Body Image Book for Boys*, a lot of boys emphasised how they were embarrassed about taking off their t-shirt at the swimming pool and generally just showing off their body.

This is something I certainly understand because again, I truly believe I will always see myself as fat and even now, I don't take off my t-shirt on holiday, in front of my parents if they want me to try on clothes they're bought me and I am seriously concerned for my future relationships to be honest.

Moreover, as I've repeatedly mentioned on the podcast before, boys and men are far less likely than women and girls to seek out help for their mental and physical health concerns. Due to a number of stupid societal and personal factors, like the outrageous belief about talking about feelings makes you weak, real men don't cry and all that other rubbish that I hate beyond words. Because it is those dumb myths that are causing so much damage to the mental health and wellbeing of our men and women in our society.

Anyway, the problem with this brand of masculinity, the type were men are only allowed to be seen as strong, stoic and independent, is that it stops them from coming forward. As well as Lynch et al. (2016) shows that recognising and having an awareness of the body image issue is the first step in obtaining treatment for it. therefore, if boys are scared of being ridiculed or stigmatised by coming forward then they will continue to try to manage their body image distress alone and I know that doesn't work.

Also I want to mention that before we move on to the last section of the podcast episode, I now know after researching this, how lucky I was and I suppose I really do need to try to be more careful about body image and try to remain positive. I think in the future, dating would help with that because that way hopefully people would tell me I'm beautiful and they like me and my body, but that is a long way off for personal and situational reasons. And again, this is just my experience, a lot of other people would have other experiences too.

Overall, this will only intensify and worsen the current mental health crisis in the teenage population, and to be honest this will kill people too.

How Do We Improve Boys' Body Image?

Now that we know how serious body image issues are and their serious consequences, we need to look at how can we solve this and start to help these boys.

Firstly, we need boys to acknowledge that they have these concerns, and this is very typical to be something that they're ashamed of. Thankfully not everyone will be ashamed of their bodies but it is okay if they are. As psychologists and therapists, we cannot do anything unless a person admits they're experiencing psychological distress and they want to change this.

Additionally, we can help these boys further to understand that body dissatisfaction is a natural reaction to have in our appearance-based culture that really does bombard us all with messages about the importance of how we look, not who we are. For example, I'm not I can actually say name of the social media site by a very famous picture-based social media site that I use loves to show my pictures of muscular men for literally no reason. I don't actually want to see these pictures but it is an example of how these pictures of "ideal" beauty and attraction are bombarded on us.

Also, we have to admit that there is a lot, a lot of money for people to make if they increase the insecurities we have about our appearance. Since these pictures could make people buy make-up, steroids, gym memberships and so many more tools we could use to achieve this ridiculously unhealthy version of "ideal" beauty. And another point to raise is why would any industry, let alone the wellness and beauty industry, stop at catering for women and girls when they could double their profits by targeting young boys and men?

It's a numbers game for sure.

Clinical Psychology Conclusion

To wrap up this podcast episode, I don't want to focus on the content this time, instead I want to focus on the message of you really are perfect the way you are. In society, we don't need to be beautiful, perfect or some messed up version of Adonis (the Greek God of beauty) and if you meet people who think that that is the only way to be then leave them. They are not going to be a healthy influence in your life, and it seriously is about time that for the sake of our mental health, the wellbeing of our young people and society as a whole that we start moving about from the appearance-based focus of our society.

We need to start understanding that everyone is perfect in their own way and that we don't all need to look like models and muscle gods or whatever the kids are called it these days. I seriously don't know what they are.

Because I can promise you this, if you don't accept yourself and if you allow body image issues to eat away inside of you then you really are playing a dangerous game. After this episode I now know I was lucky I was a few years ago but a lot of other people aren't so lucky.

So please be careful, accept yourself and have the body that *you* want. Not what something else wants you to have.

Clinical Psychology References

Glazer, K. B., Ziobrowski, H. N., Horton, N. J., Calzo, J. P., & Field, A. E. (2021). The course of weight/shape concerns and disordered eating symptoms among adolescent and young adult males. *Journal of Adolescent Health*, *69*(4), 615-621.

https://www.nationaleatingdisorders.org/busting-myths-about-eating-disorders

Lynch, L., Long, M., & Moorhead, A. (2018). Young Men, Help-Seeking, and Mental Health Services: Exploring Barriers and Solutions. *American journal of men's health*, *12*(1), 138–149. https://doi.org/10.1177/1557988315619469

Markey, C., Hart, D., & Zacher, D. (2022). *Being You: The Body Image Book for Boys*. Cambridge University Press.

McLean, S. A., Wertheim, E. H., & Paxton, S. J. (2018). Preferences for being muscular and thin in 6-year-old boys. *Body image*, *26*, 98-102.

MODELS OF EATING DISORDERS

As psychology students and professionals, we know that psychology loves to create models to explain how different psychological processes and mental health conditions are developed and maintained by a client. Sometimes these models are great, some are okay and some models (like the Multistore Model Memory) you can just tell are a little too simplistic to actually explain how these processes work in reality.

When it comes to eating disorders there are a range of models that psychologists can draw on, and that is what we're going to look at now.

<u>The Tripartite Model</u>

This model designed to explain eating disorders comes from two studies, van den Berg, Thompson, Obremski & Coovert, (2002) as well as Yamamiya, Shroff & Thompson (2006). This model proposes that eating disorders happen because of three main types of factors that cause the condition to develop and become maintained.

Firstly, peer influences are a massive factor when it comes to eating disorders because adolescent girls tend to learn their attitudes about dieting as well as slimness from their peers (Levine et al., 1994). This leads to people adopting unhealthy weight control behaviour, like self-induced vomiting, and these behaviours are influenced by their friends (Story & Perry, 2005).

Sometimes this influence is very subtle for example you might get a client with a group of friends that are all skinny and they constantly talk about the importance of being skinny. Then the client themselves might not be to their friends' level of skinyness so they looking for tips and tricks so they can get down to their friends' weight and ideals.

Equally, the social influence can sadly be more overt at times where groups of friends openly encourage and talk about these weight control behaviours, and they do it together.

Another type of social influence comes from family factors because eating disorders tend to run in families. That's why when it comes to the treatment of eating disorders, they are often best understood by considering family dynamics (Minuchin et al., 1975). Especially as the person with the eating disorder could be embedded in a dysfunctional family structure that actively promotes them developing an eating disorder.

This is good to remember because eating disorders can be a control thing too. Sometimes people develop an eating disorder because what they eat is the only thing in their life that they can control, and this lack of control that the person feels is mainly down to social factors like family dynamics.

Secondly, if you've looked at clinical psychology and cognitive behavioural therapy before then you might be familiar with predisposing factors, and these are factors that makes a person more likely to develop a condition. Think about these as risk factors if you will.

Therefore, when it comes to eating disorders, there is evidence that life stresses, negative emotions, lack of social support and the internalisation of a thin ideal body image as risk factors for developing an eating disorder.

In addition, Serpell and Troop (2003) found that if a person experiences helplessness or adversity has a child, has low self-esteem and/or rigour perfectionism then these personality factors increase their vulnerability of developing eating disorders.

It is always good to have research on risk and predisposing factors so we can watch and monitor people that are most at risk. Then in an ideal world, we would be able to help them as soon as they start showing signs of developing an eating disorder, because if you catch it early before the negative automatic thoughts have come too entrenched then this might make them easier to treat.

Overall, it is psychological factors, like a person's high levels of shyness, perfectionism, low self-esteem, high introspective awareness, dependence and non-assertiveness and negative or depressed moods that increases a person's chance of developing an eating disorder.

Experiential Factors

Finally, this model looks at how a person's experiences and observations impact their chances of developing an eating disorder, because people with anorexia and bulimia report having more negative life experiences than healthy controls (Rastam & Gillberg, 1991; Welch et al., 1997).

Additionally, these same clinical populations have higher incidence rates of childhood sexual abuse (Brown et al., 1997; Steiger et al., 2000) but these increased rates aren't found in people with binge eating disorder.

This helps to explain why eating disorders become a coping mechanism. It is still a maladaptive one but it is important to the person nonetheless. Hence, why CBT is needed to help them find a more adaptive coping mechanism to deal with the past.

CBT Models

Since this is an introduction to CBT book, I couldn't have a chapter on psychological models without talking about CBT, so we need to talk about Fairburn (1997)'s Cognitive Model Of Bulimia.

Of course, this might be easier to explain with a

diagram but that has too many formatting problems for me to be able to do that.

Therefore, the model proposes that Bulimia is caused by and maintained by a person having low self-esteem and having extreme concerns about their shape and weight, and then this leads to them following a strict dieting. But the strict diet makes them hungry so they binge eat, then because they still have these extreme concerns they take part in self-induced vomiting and other purging behaviours.

All these factors are interconnected and impacted each other.

Personally, I do rather like this model because it does address a lot of cognitive aspects, but the problem with all of these models is that they aren't very holistic, because this model fails to explain how the social influence interact with the cognitive factors to cause and maintain an eating disorder.

<u>Transdiagnostic Models Of Eating Disorders</u>

Lastly for this chapter, as I mentioned earlier in the book, there are times when a person has an eating disorder and another mental health condition or conditions. This is very problematic for therapists because normal CBT and other CBT models are designed to work with only one condition.

For example, CBT for depression is only designed to work for depression, not anxiety. CBT for eating disorders is designed for eating disorders, not depression or anxiety.

Therefore, when a client does have one or more

mental health conditions in addition to an eating disorder, the psychologist would need to make a choice about what to treat first. Since a client's depression could be maintaining the eating disorder, because the eating disorder could be a coping mechanism with the low mood, or vice versa. The client might have depression because they have extreme concerns about their weight.

What would do treat first?

It is always a tough question.

That's why transdiagnostic models are so important in modern clinical psychology, and I'm really pleased that there is always research being conducted on them. Due to these models look at the common processes or maintaining factors common across all eating disorders, and there are models being developed to treat eating disorders and non-eating disorders together if needed.

For example, Fairburn (2008) and Fairburn et al. (2013) created the Transdiagnostic cognitive-behavioural model, which focuses on the dysfunctional sense of self evaluation that is central to all eating disorders, how self-worth is defined by a client as control over their weight, shape and eating behaviours. Then the model looks at how this leads to dietary restraint, which is maintained by their perfectionism, mood intolerance and low self-esteem.

How all these different factors are treated will be explored now so let's start exploring treatment options for these conditions.

PART TWO: TREATMENT FOR EATING DISORDERS

CBT FOR EATING DISORDERS AND BODY DYSMORPHIC DISORDER

INTRODUCTION TO THE TREATMENT OF EATING DISORDERS

Moving onto the next section of the book, we're now going to be talking about the treatment side of eating disorders, because now that we know how deadly, concerning and scary these mental health conditions are. We need to understand how we can possibly start to treat them.

Cognitive Behavioural Maintaining Factors

When it comes to treatment we need to understand that Cognitive Behavioural Therapy focuses on the cognitive and behavioural approach and combines them. In the two other CBT books, I've explained what each of these approaches are in depth, but to summarise these psychological approaches, the cognitive approaches proposes that mental health conditions are caused by maladaptive coping mechanisms that are formed by the person to protect themselves from the psychological distress caused by their biased cognitive processes.

Whereas behavioural approaches propose that mental health conditions and the symptoms of them are the results of learnt behaviours, and the central tenant of the approach is that if something is learnt, it can be unlearnt.

I would love it if mental health conditions were that simple.

Anyway, we already know that people could be vulnerable to developing eating disorders because of both personal and environmental predisposing factors. As well as once a person has an eating disorder, this condition is maintained by both cognitive and behavioural factors (Fairburn, 2008).

For example, this includes negative beliefs like, "I'm worthless", "I'm unlovable" and "I'm unattractive".

As a result of these maintaining factors, these make a person develop assumptions about themselves and these might not have a major effect on a person until they're activated by stresses in adolescence and early adulthood.

Therefore, when these core beliefs and assumptions about themselves, others and the world are triggered in a specific trigger context, this leads to a range of negative automatic thoughts relating to dieting.

For instance, in anorexia, these core beliefs and assumptions lead a person to restrict their eating and this is maintained by the sense of self-worth and control it gives them. As well as peer group and family approval could also reinforce these beliefs.

These are all things that need to be worked on during therapy.

As a result, these biased, negative cognitions lead to a range of associated behaviours that contribute to the maintenance of the eating disorder as well. These include:
- Mirror checking
- Checking of body part by touch
- Camouflaging
- Other safety behaviours and avoidance behaviours
- Appearance comparison

Treatment For Eating Disorders

Whilst I talk more about the clinical assessment and interview in CBT For Depression, I do want to give you a little run down here so you can have a good understanding.

The first step of any psychological treatment is the full clinical interview and when it comes to CBT, there is one main model that always springs to mind for me whenever I talk about it or learn about this topic, and that is the 5P Model of CBT. If you've done clinical psychology before then at this point I sort of liken it to seeing an old friend again, because the 5P model is always your friend and it will never leave you. But if you haven't done clinical psychology before then you are in for a treat.

The 5P model is based on the idea that a client

has 5 factors or facets of their mental health condition that you can use to inform your formulation and then this in turn helps a therapist to decide what intervention to use. Or to be honest, how to make CBT a little more targeted for this particular client.

The five facets are:

- Presenting issues- focusing on the here and now
- Precipitating factors focusing on what triggered the condition recently
- Predisposing factors- focusing on things in the past
- Perpetuating factors- known as a vicious cycle or what maintains the condition
- Protective factors- a client's strengths and personal resources

Now even though, as therapists (future or current) we might not be interested at all at first in protective factors, this is a massive mistake because we need to see protective factors as things that are just as important as how the condition is manifesting. Since we can help our client to see how brilliant, strong and resilient they are by pointing out all their strengths and resources.

This is even more important when we consider how eating disorders leads to biased cognitive processes that makes the person believe not eating and having a clinically normal relationship with food gives them a sense of control and self-worth.

In addition, since eating disorders are very serious and deadly, there are other steps that need to be taken too in psychological treatment. For example, their weight and height need to be taken so their BMI can be calculated, or if dealing with a person under 18 then their height centile is taken. Remember eating disorders can stunt or negatively impact development in children so height is another good indicator.

Also, the psychologist would find out the person's weight trajectory, or in other words their average weight loss/gain per week.

All before the client has to take part in a number of psychometric tests. For example, everyone has to do the Eating Disorder Examination Questionnaire but if the adolescent is under 14 then they have to do a specific version for that age group. As well as there are medical checks involved that come from baseline measures from a doctor, including the testing of blood electrolytes, because this is something that is heavily negatively impacted by restriction of diet.

Other rating and psychometric tests are include:

- Eating Disorders Inventory-3
- The Children's Eating Attitudes Test
- Morgan-Russell Average Outcome Scale (MRAOS)
- Bulimic Investigatory Test (BITE)

Overall, the entire aim of an assessment is multiple. Due to the psychologist needs to understand if the person does have an eating disorder. For example, does the person have a morbid fear of fatness and the associated shape weight and size cognitions?

In addition, they need to decide what is the most

appropriate treatment for this particular person or family. Remember formulation is about tailoring the psychotherapy to the individual because no one is the same meaning no treatment is identical.

Finally, the aims of an assessment are to see if the person has the motivation to change or engage in the therapy process. That is seriously a massive predictor of success and without that engagement or drive then it is honestly close to pointless. As well as if there isn't engagement then could this motivation be enhanced through the family?

For the sake of the client I seriously hope so, but it sadly isn't always possible.

Risk Assessment In Eating Disorders

However, I know throughout the book so far I've stressed how deadly, serious and scary eating disorders are, that's why risk assessments are critical steps in the therapy process too. Since psychologists and the multi-disciplinary team around the client need to treat the physical symptoms and the psychological symptoms.

In other words, they have to treat the extreme thinness and the negative cognitive processes that make the extreme thinness a "good" thing in the client's mind.

Therefore, when it comes to anorexia, the team need to know what the client's current daily food and liquid intake is, what is their weight loss timeline (for example did the weight loss start three months ago, six months or whatever and how much weight has been loss in this time), and they need to know about menstruation.

Other information the team need to know from the client includes:

- Collateral information about consequences
- What are the client's highest, lowest, and preferred weight?
- Does the client use any alcohol, drugs or medications?
- What are their purging behaviours? Like vomiting, compulsive exercise, laxatives, diet pills.
- Do they do body-checking and avoidance behaviours?
- Are they socially withdrawn and/ or have social conflict?
- Do they have any physical diseases? For example, thyrotoxicosis, diabetes, bowel disease cystic fibrosis and malignancies.

Overall, psychologists and the treatment team have to get a hell of a lot of information to inform their formulations and their assessment. This is critical because not only does that allow them to understand the condition or what the client is experiencing as fully as humanly possible, but it gives them as much information as they can so they can make an informed decision about what the best treatment option is.

That's good because we talk about a wide range of treatments in the next few chapters and not all of them are good for everyone, some people will prefer and respond better to CBT, others family therapy and others sadly won't at all.

As a result, if we take anorexia, then the psychologist and team need to consider issues and problems in the treatment as well. Since it is a challenge to manage the client's physical risk, because normally, we only have to bear in mind the client's mental state and psychological states, but in the treatment of eating disorders, biological factors are more important than normal.

For example, the client losing more than 1 kilogram a week, that is a scary factor because if a client loses too much weight then they will die. That's why psychotherapy doesn't really start for a client until they're a more reasonable weight.

As well as psychologists have to consider issues around the client's purging behaviours, substance use and how physical weakness in clients have to be tube feed.

Furthermore, there are behavioural risks to manage too. For instance, the consequences of starvation on a child's developing brain and cognition, as well as the urgency to refeeding underweight children. As well as the importance of family and caregiver education, especially if they're a maintaining factor. That's why family-based therapy, not always CBT can be useful.

But the assessment is just a starting point and

treatment cannot start without it.

So what are some of these treatment options I keep mentioning?

TREATMENT AND ISSUES RELATED TO ENGAGEMENT

Continuing with our investigation into how eating disorders are treated, now that we have a basic foundation of treatments that will be built on in future chapters, we need to talk about some issues.

Since the biggest problem with people with eating disorders is that they don't believe they have mental health difficulties or faulty thinking patterns. They think their extreme dieting and purging behaviour is healthy and everyone should do it.

That is just one reason why eating disorders are hard to treat.

<u>Issues Relating To Engagement</u>

The common challenges that therapists face in treating eating disorders is, of course, the client's ambivalence to the deadliness of their condition, so this is why there's a massive need to emphasise the process of engagement within therapy.

If you've done clinical psychology before then

you might be familiar with the therapeutic alliance and why the relationship between the therapist and client is so important for the success of the therapy.

One model that is useful in dealing with this challenge comes from Miller and Rollnick (2012) who proposed the Stages of Change Model, saying that therapeutic change happens in the following stages:

- Pre-contemplation
- Contemplation
- Preparation
- Action
- Maintenance

In other words, the model proposes that our clients need to willingly contemplate therapeutic change first before they could ever hope to prepare for this change, take action so the change can happen and follow the therapy steps so the change can be maintained.

Then because that model is very theoretical and not at all useful at first in the therapy room, a therapist could implement this stage by using motivational interviewing. This helps the client to move from the precontemplation and contemplation stages to preparation action and maintenance stages, as you're motivating them to change.

Prevention

In an ideal world, we wouldn't have to treat eating disorders with highly specialist therapists with very technical mental health teams, because if there is more time and money invested into prevention programmes then a lot of people wouldn't develop these deadly conditions in the first place.

Therefore, prevention work for eating disorders is typically done in groups at clinics, athletic clubs and schools with targeted programs being more effective. As well as this prevention work typically involves having a minimum Body Mass Index for dancers and models so this decreases the perceived need to be extremely thin, anti-obesity campaigns and work that emphasises healthy nutrition and exercise rather than weight reduction are all important messages in preventing eating disorders.

When it comes to the programmes themselves, school-based prevention programmes emphasise the role that the media plays in promoting extreme body ideals (this is showed in another chapter in more depth), why children need to develop a positive body image, have a healthy, balanced diet as well as develop the skills associated with expressing feelings and combating depression.

All of these factors are important when we remember why eating disorders develop in the first place as a coping mechanism of control and to combat negative emotions.

Some prevention programmes include, Body Project (Stice et al. 2012) and Healthy Weight (Srice et al 2003).

Difficulties In Treating Eating Disorders

As I mentioned earlier, a lot of people with

eating disorders deny they have one and people with severe eating disorders often receive medical treatment prior to psychological interventions. As well as like we saw earlier, it's sadly common for eating disorders to be comorbid with another mental health condition and only makes the required treatment more complex.

I will admit that by the end of the book, you will realise at a deep level how complex eating disorders and similar conditions are to treat. Since there is a lack of capacity to change on the side of the client and there are a lot of biological factors to focus on. I mean that you cannot start treatment at all until the client is at a survivable and healthy weight. That takes time.

And in a way when it comes to eating disorders, it isn't the thoughts that will kill the client immediately. It is the biological impact of starvation that the thoughts cause that will kill the client long before therapy begins to make good progress.

That is the tragic reality of eating disorders.

Self-Help & Alternative Delivery Systems

Personally, I am always very nervous talking about self-help stuff because I don't always agree with it, and to be honest, because eating disorders are so deadly, I flat out disagree with self-help here. Professional help is the only way.

However, I always want to give you readers as much information as possible. Therefore, there are self-help routes for eating disorders, including self-help groups, but CBT and psychological therapies aren't the only way to treat eating disorders.

Due to treatment and support for these conditions can be delivered over the phone, internet and email, as well as computer software, like CD-ROMs (I barely remember those things).

My point is thankfully there are a lot of options available for treating eating disorders, but CBT is the best one and I do prefer it.

Leading us onto the all important question of what are the psychological treatments for eating disorders?

PSYCHOLOGICAL TREATMENT FOR EATING DISORDERS

As we start to turn our attention towards the psychological methods used in treating eating disorders before focusing on Cognitive Behavioural Therapy for the rest of this section of the book, I want to quickly mention some pharmacological treatments.

Interestingly enough, antidepressants are the most common form of drug treatment for eating disorders with there being some evidence that this treatment can reduce bulimia symptoms (e.g. Bellini & Merli, 2004).

Now as always what I find interesting about biological methods for psychological conditions is that pharmacological treatments aren't effective in the long term considering that a person's drive for thinness and extreme dieting isn't biological in nature, it is psychological. Therefore, biological treatments will never ever be able to help a person come up with more adaptive coping mechanisms for their psychological thoughts and drives.

Additionally, pharmacological treatments with anorexia have tended to be less successful (Pederson et al., 2003).

However, it's important to know that antidepressant treatments for eating disorders do have significantly higher relapse and drop-out rates than psychological interventions. Again this comes back to drug treatments failing and being useless at targeting the psychological causes of a condition.

As a result, the best outcomes for eating disorders are when drug treatments are combined with CBT programmes.

Family Therapy

If we cast our minds back to a few chapters ago then I mentioned how family factors have a role in how eating disorders are maintained and developed in the first place, for that reason family therapy can be an effective way to treat eating disorders.

Also, this is one of the most common interventions used with eating disorders with the therapy being based on the idea that eating disorders hide important conflicts within the family.

Personally, I do enjoy systemic therapy because the idea of the family as a system is very useful and utterly fascinating. Of course, systemic theory doesn't look at everything and it does miss out on psychological factors, but it is still interesting.

And there is no such thing as a perfect theory in clinical psychology.

Cognitive Behavioural Therapy

CBT is the treatment of choice when it comes to eating disorders and even more so for (Wilson & Shafran, 2005) with this form of CBT being based on the cognitive model we looked at earlier developed by Fairburn et al. (1999). Since people with bulimia develop negative evaluations about themselves and have idealized beliefs about thinness, as well as distorted views of their own body shape.

All these areas and beliefs are challenged during a course of CBT and there is an Enhanced form of CBT that is used as well, and there's a whole chapter dedicated to that form coming up next. CBT is really helpful for clients that are significantly underweight too.

What Are The Stages Of CBT For Bulimia?

We'll this in more depth in a moment, but the four stages of CBT For Bulimia according to Fairburn (1985) are:

- Psychoeducation about the effects of purging, bingeing and mood.
- Modified eating patterns – small meals 5-6 times a day instead of bingeing to start off with.
- Altering the client's dysfunctional attitudes about food, eating and the body.
- Teaching the client coping strategies to avoid bingeing & purging.

When a person with bulimia first starts CBT, the

focus will be meal planning and stimulus control so instead of snacking and binge eating, the meals can be controlled more so they eat properly three times a day, or whatever the therapist deems appropriate.

Furthermore, cognitive restructuring is a core part of CBT so when it comes to Bulimia, this is used to address the client's dysfunctional beliefs about their body shape and weight.

Then the focus shifts to become focused on developing relapse prevention methods so the eating disorder doesn't return after therapy ends.

Overall, CBT for eating disorders is based on identifying the dysfunctional thinking processes that cause and maintain the disordered eating, as well as using behavioural exercises to test and modify these maladaptive beliefs.

CBT For Anorexia Nervosa

Whereas CBT For Anorexia focuses on different clinical features, because we know from other chapters that anorexia involves several cognitive distortions. For instance, the client has irrational beliefs about weight gain and good and they have an inaccurate perception of their body.

Therefore, this form of CBT aims to change these faulty thinking patterns, which the therapy assumes is what maintains the anorexic behaviour.

Now what makes this form of CBT so special is that if you think normal CBT is highly structured then this is even more so. Due to CBT for Anorexia is the most effective treatment we have at this point for short-term clients.

Although, if the client needs psychological help in the longer term then they might benefit more from family therapy or Interpersonal Psychotherapy.

Overall, whilst that was a quick whistle-stop tour of CBT for eating disorders, our next chapter focuses a lot more on Enhanced Cognitive-Behavioural Therapy for eating disorders (Fairburn, 2008) and it might be my favourite chapter out of the entire book.

CBT FOR EATING DISORDERS AND BODY DYSMORPHIC DISORDER

WHAT IS ENHANCED COGNITIVE BEHAVIOURAL THERAPY?

As we move onto the treatment part of Eating Disorders, I wanted to share with you this great psychology article that I originally wrote for The Psychology World Podcast. Yet I wanted to add it here because it serves as an excellent guide to E-CBT and whilst we expand on this information in the next chapter even more. This article is a brilliant introduction and guide to E-CBT.

Personally, I found this section fascinating so I know you will too.

Enjoy!

***

As this podcast is mainly for psychology students and professionals, we should have all heard about cognitive behavioural therapy, what is it and why it is so effective at treating a wide range of mental health conditions. As well as different forms of cognitive behavioural therapy have been adapted to treat different conditions, like psychosis, and now we'll going to look at a different form of cognitive behavioural therapy that focuses on treating Eating Disorders. This is going to be a great podcast episode that is absolutely perfect for anyone interested in mental health, clinical psychology and eating disorders.

Introduction To Enhanced Cognitive Behavioural Therapy

As many of us know, Cognitive Behavioural Therapy (CBT) is a very popular and extremely well-researched psychotherapy that is highly effective at treating a wide range of mental health conditions. For example, depression, OCD, anxiety amongst a bunch of other conditions. As well as CBT focuses on identifying a client's patterns of thoughts, emotions and/ or the behaviours that negatively impact and influence their lives.

As a result of its effectiveness, CBT has been adapted into different forms to treat different conditions more effectively. Including Enhanced CBT (CBT-E) that is focused on treating eating disorders, and this will the focus of this brilliant podcast episode.

What Is CBT-E?

When it comes to treating eating disorders, like Anorexia (AN), Binge Eating Disorder (BED) and Bulimia Nervosa (BN), CBT-E is considered a first-line and evidence-based treatment for these conditions amongst other eating disorders. And even though, these conditions present us, as current or future, psychologists with very different problematic behaviours, they all share the same foundational features at their very core. Such as people with Anorexia, BED and Bulimia, they all often experience extreme concerns with their weight, body shape and/or find it difficult to cope with negative emotions.

These factors lead to a client to "overvalue" their body shape and weight and mood intolerance, all of which are common triggers to problematic eating behaviours. Such as binge eating, purging and food restriction.

Therefore, CBT-E is a very structured and manualised treatment like other forms of CBT, that is intended to fit the client "like a glove" by focusing on creating a personalised map or formulation of the client's eating disorder in order to create a customised plan for addressing the unique patterns and challenges.

Personally, this is why I love formulation so much, because it is so critical and important when it comes to mental health conditions. Since you can have two clients with the exact same eating disorder, but you cannot treat them exactly the same, because each other will have their own backgrounds, histories and social and psychological factors that can be causing the maladaptive coping mechanisms. And that's why creating a formulation that is personalised to the client is so critical.

However, CBT-E isn't a first-line approach for adolescents and children with anorexia or bulimia. In these cases, it is very common for treatments for children and teenagers with eating disorders to incorporate caregivers either as a central part of the treatment or very closely integrated. Since Family-based treatment is a far more common recommendation for younger people presenting with disordered eating.

What Are The Four Stages of CBT-E?

In terms of practicalities, there are four stages of CBT-E that are done over the course of 20 to 40 weeks using regular outpatient therapy sessions. Normally not a lot of clients reach the 40 week mark since this is only really for clients who need to restore their weight like clients with anorexia nervosa. As well as CBT-E highlights to clients the importance of "starting well" and building as much momentum at the start of therapy as they can, so sessions are normally twice a week for the first four to eight weeks, then they drop down to once a week for eight weeks and then go every-other-week afterwards.

And I know I was surprised when I learnt that therapy sessions were twice a week at the start so I think others will be too. Yet there are a range of reasons for this, but one of them has to be that eating disorders are extremely deadly conditions as we've spoken about before. Therefore, it is critical to try to build as much momentum in the early parts of the therapy just to try and give the therapy as much chance of working as possible.

Stage One of CBT-E

The entire point of stage one is about understanding and then systematically addressing the factors that keep the client locked into their eating difficulties. To do this the therapy would guide the client in establishing a pattern of consistent as well as regular eating, and the client would learn how to effectively plan ahead, anticipate challenges and maintain a predictable routine of eating every few hours.

Additionally, this first stage involves a lot of building self-awareness, education and problem-solving for the client to help them avoid known triggers. Then the therapist would expect significant change during this brief first stage of the first four to eight weeks.

Stage Two Of CBT-E

Secondly, stage two is only a session or two where the client and therapist reviews progression, collaborate on building a plan for Stage Three and identify any ongoing challenges.

What Is Stage Three of CBT-E?

Now Stage Three occurs during the once-a-week sessions and they focus on factors that could be fuelling the remaining problematic eating behaviours. These are typically concerned with body shape and weight. Also a lot of attention at this stage is focused on forms of over-control of food, like the types of food that a client continues to avoid, the restriction of their overall food intake and more.

Overall, stage three focuses on the mood and event-related triggers of a client's disordered eating.

What Is Stage Four Of CBT-E?

Finally, the fourth and final stage focus on the therapist and the client looking ahead to the future and life after CBT-E. Therefore, the client learns about consistency, mindfulness and how to engage strategies to reduce the vulnerability of them relapsing in the future.

Barriers To Treatment and Barriers To CBT-E

I always like to offset therapy-based podcast episodes by highlighting the immense problems that some amazing future-clients have when it comes to accessing therapy. I mainly do this because I want to help raise awareness so hopefully these barriers can be ripped down in the future. And yes, sometimes I really am that much of an optimist.

When it comes to CBT-E, there are a number of barriers that prove very problematic for people because CBT-E is very expensive and it isn't accessible to a lot of people. Especially in countries like the USA where they don't have free healthcare, as well as from what I've read it seems to be difficult to find CBT-E providers that accept commercial insurance or Medicaid.

Additionally, and please note this is NOT an official recommendation from me in any way, shape or form, but I have read a few experts recommend the book *Overcoming Binge Eating* By Christopher Fairburn by saying that his self-help guide can be used as an effective course for BED and sometimes BN, as well as it could be more effective if there was external support available as a supplement.

But again, I am NOT recommending that book officially.

Thankfully, there are some specialised eating disorder training and research centres that offer CBT-E at a reduced rate or even free of charge in exchange for participation in research studies. That is brilliant in my opinion, but this is a major problem that still needs to be fixed in society.

Clinical Psychology Conclusion

I will never deny that eating disorders are extremely deadly mental health conditions and treating the people with these conditions is beyond critical. I know I occasionally mention that psychotherapy saves lives, but in this case, I truly, truly mean it.

And as current or future psychologists, we need to acknowledge that what we do has amazing power and is a force of good for people and their lives, so just remember that when you're down or having a rough time.

Because you truly never know what positive impact you'll have on someone in their darkest hour.

Clinical Psychology and Eating Disorder References

Atwood, M.E., Friedman, A. (2019). A systematic

review of enhanced cognitive behavioral therapy (CBT-E) for eating disorders. *International Journal of Eating Disorders*, 53(3), 311-330.

https://www.cbte.co/what-is-cbte/a-description-of-cbt-e/

Murphy R, Straebler S, Cooper Z, Fairburn CG. Cognitive behavioral therapy for eating disorders. Psychiatr Clin North Am. 2010 Sep;33(3):611-27. doi: 10.1016/j.psc.2010.04.004. PMID: 20599136; PMCID: PMC2928448.

E-CBT FOCUSING ON BULIMIA

Now that we know from the last chapter what E-CBT involves at a more general level, I want to expand on this in this final chapter on Eating Disorders by focusing and applying E-CBT knowledge to Bulimia specifically.

In addition, the typical session format of E-CBT is typically 50 minutes long and we know this involves in-session weigh-ins and you review the homework and assignments like in other forms of CBT, like I spoke about in CBT For Depression. As well as the psychologist and client collaboratively work together to develop the session's agenda and specific intervention.

That's definitely one of the things that I love about CBT is that it is so collaborative and it really is a process *with* our client and this has additional therapeutic benefits.

Stage 1: Collaborative Formulation

Focusing on Bulimia, we know from earlier chapters that a person's binge eating is identified as a core concern and the client might propose dieting as a solution but this maintains binge eating and it contributes to feelings of intense hunger and negative emotions. Leading to binge eating because in the short term binge eating does reduce negative emotional states.

But in Bulimia, purging and vomiting behaviours also maintain binge eating behaviour. As a result, the client has a belief that if they reduce their weight then this will lead to improved self-worth and this promotes extreme dieting.

Therefore, the client and the therapist will need to work on a few different areas for the therapy to work.

Firstly, the client and therapist must work on psychoeducation. This involves the therapist talking to the client about information regarding how Body Mass Index is calculated and what is considered normal by BMI standards.

Also, a client needs to understand at a deep level that having a target weight doesn't have to involve dieting and it shouldn't. then the therapist would need to explain the psychological and physical effects of vomiting, self-starving and bingeing. As well as get the client to understand how dieting contributes to their feelings of loss of control, intense hunger and bingeing.

Another area of this first stage of therapy involves self-monitoring sheets were the client records what they eat each day at what time and place and whether this was viewed as binging, and whether this meal or food was followed by purging, laxative use or vomiting behaviours.

This is really important in treating eating disorders because this gives the therapist a lot of information about how the client lives and their mental health difficulties surrounding eating. Then this has the added benefit of allowing the client to see their own habits and how this isn't healthy.

After the psychologist has this information, they can start working with the client about stimulus control, developing alternative behaviours to bingeing and vomiting. As well as they can address the problematic patterns of excessive exercise, diuretic and laxative use.

Also, it is worth noting that this formulation does tend to involve significant others and partners at this stage of the treatment. Especially as we learnt earlier that people with eating disorders don't see themselves as having a mental health condition and they don't always see the negatives of their behaviour.

Stage 2

Like in all eating disorders, in Stage 2 of E-CBT for Bulimia, the psychologist and client would take stock by reviewing the client's progress, reformulate if needed (which it always is) and plan the next stage of the therapy by developing a specific treatment plan.

Stage 3

Now that the therapist and the client with Bulimia have that treatment plan, Stage 3 is continuing with the Stage 1 processes by improving the client's problem solving so they don't feel like they have to binge to improve their mood and the client reduces dieting behaviour.

Also, like all CBT therapies, the client's maladaptive cognitive distortions are challenged and helped, with the main elements of this stage being interventions that focus on the client's over-evaluation of their body weight and shape and their sense of control. Since these are the main factors that maintain the Eating Disorder.

This is typically done by increasing the importance of other areas of a client's self-evaluation, and addressing their body checking and avoidance behaviours.

In case the "increasing importance of other areas" strategy wasn't clear. In Social Psychology, we talk about how there are different parts of our self-esteem and we value these different parts of our self-esteem in different ways. For example, I highly value the parts of myself that are a psychology student, author and podcaster, but I value my cooking and gardening and reader part of myself less.

For people with eating disorders, they highly value their thinness and other maladaptive parts of themselves that help them maintain their eating disorder, but they might value their social and daughter self less. Therefore, in therapy, you might want to increase how important the client sees their social self to replace the importance of their thinness. That's an example.

Furthermore, at this stage of the therapy, the psychologist would work on strategies to control the "eating disorder mindset" by exploring the development of the over-evaluation of shape and weight and their control in the first place to see why the client has this need.

However, there are other strategies used too. For instance, working on the client's mood tolerance to help them not feel low in the first place and then there isn't that drive to binge eating to improve their mood. The strategies used to help develop a tolerance for negative states is based on Dialectical Behaviour Therapy (DBT).

Also, the client would attempt to address the strict rules they have about eating and they would be encouraged to have a regular eating pattern.

Stage 4 Relapse Prevention And Additional Stage Two Modules For Intensive CBT

Finally, as you saw in the last chapter, stage 4 of E-CBT is all about relapse prevention and this involves 3 sessions every two weeks. Then if this is intensive E-CBT then the client has modules and sessions on addressing perfectionism because they might be obsessed with having the "perfect" body. As well as addressing core low self-esteem.

Something I do want to point out is that I really enjoy how CBT is structured so you can adapt it for different mental health conditions and that's critical. CBT for Eating Disorders isn't perfect but it really tries and really addresses a lot of concerns and factors that maintain eating disorders.

And that's what makes CBT so fascinating to look at.

However, as we finish up eating disorders, we now need to investigate how harmful, deadly and concerning one mental health condition is that has parrels with eating disorders. So let's turn over the page and start exploring Body Dysmorphia Disorder.

PART THREE: BODY DYSMORPHIA DISORDER

CBT FOR EATING DISORDERS AND BODY DYSMORPHIC DISORDER

INRTODUCTION TO BODY DYSMORPHIA DISORDER

Kicking off the third section of the book and investigating the next mental health condition this book aims to cover, we now need to talk about Body Dysmorphic Disorder, but please know that for the rest of the book because it is a lot easier to type out (and it is another term for it) Body Dysmorphia will be used.

This is a very interesting condition that is comparable to eating disorders in the sense that it impacts how a person sees their body shape and weight, but that is basically where the comparison ends.

Also, in this section, we expand the CBT knowledge and information you'll receive more.

Therefore, this condition can be traced back to Morselli (1886) where the term Dysmorphophobia was used to describe the following:

"Subjective feeling of ugliness or physical defect

which the patient feels is noticeable to others, although the appearance is within normal limits. The patient is really miserable in the middle of his daily routines, while talking, while reading, during meals, everywhere and at anytime, he is caught by the doubt of deformity".

Leading us to the modern Body Dysmorphic Disorder and according to the DSM-5 (APA, 2013), this is a mental health condition that makes a person have a preoccupation with one or more perceived flaws or defects in their physical appearance, and it's very important to know that these flaws or defects cannot be observable or they only appear as slight flaws to others.

For example, if a person who was badly hurt in a fire regarded their facial burns as defects then chances are this person wouldn't have body dysmorphia, because the flaws are real and they can get seen by others. Granted it is still probably a good idea that the burn victim gets some help about reframing her burns because they could be causing her some psychological distress, but this isn't enough for a diagnosis of body dysmorphia.

Whereas if a person had a minor mould on their chin that is the size of a raisin and they thought this mole made them the worse looking person ever and they were going to die alone because of it. Then chances are they would have body dysmorphia.

See the difference.

In addition, body dysmorphia comes under the classification category of obsessive compulsive and related disorders in the DSM. Since at some point during the course of the condition, a person will perform repetitive behaviours or mental acts in response to their appearance concerns.

Also, like all mental health conditions, a diagnosis can only be achieved if the preoccupation caused by body dysmorphia causes the client clinically significant levels of distress and/ or impairment in social, occupational or other important areas of functioning.

Nonetheless, the real difference between eating disorders and body dysmorphia is that a person's preoccupation with their body shape and weight isn't better explained by any concerns they have with body fat or weight in that would match the symptoms in the diagnostic criteria for an eating disorder.

Also, like most conditions, there is a range of body dysmorphia from someone having a good insight into the reality of the flaw. Like they realise they have big concerns about their "defect" but they realise it isn't going to destroy their life. All the way up to the client being delusional about the defect.

What About The ICD-11?

Whilst there aren't too many differences between the DSM-5 and the ICD-11 by the World Health Organisation (2018), because both manuals admit body dysmorphia is a persistent preoccupation with one or more perceived defects or flaws in a person's appearance that are either unnoticeable or only slightly noticeable to others.

The difference is that the ICD-11 adds that the person with body dysmorphia experiences excessive self-consciousness about their defect, as well as in response to this preoccupation, people engage in excessive and repetitive behaviours.

Then it stresses the importance of the preoccupation causing the person clinically significant levels of distress and impairment.

Location Of "Defect" In Body Dysmorphia

People with body dysmorphia tend to have a lot of different concerns about their body. It is rarely just one concern, like one ear being slightly bigger than the other, or their nose being the "wrong" shape and the like.

Typically, the most common "defects" are to do with the face. For example, a person with body dysmorphia will have problems with their teeth, chin, lips, nose, facial skin, hair, eyes or they sadly believe that they have an ugly face in general.

Yet any part of their body could be the focus of their preoccupation.

Additionally, an extreme preoccupation isn't the only symptom of body dysmorphia due to mirror checking and other body checking are symptoms as well.

Moreover, to the other safety and avoidance behaviours the person uses, more on that later on.

Such as their distorted self-image and self-focus, their appearance comparison, their seeking out of dermatological or cosmetic treatment or surgery.

Prevalence, Demographics, Impact On Life And Aetiology

In terms of how common body dysmorphia is, we need to look at Veale et al. (2016) who conducted a Systematic review of studies and found the following prevalence rates for body dysmorphia: 3.3% of students had body dysmorphia, 1.9% of adults and 2.2% of adolescents would have the condition, as well as 5.8% adult psychiatric out-patients have the condition too.

Then when gender was included, women were more likely than men to develop body dysmorphia. As well as the weighted prevalence was used in the study to control for other factors.

Overall, as you can see after taking out psychiatric out-patients, women and young people were most likely to develop body dysmorphia.

Why Should We Care?

I always like to cover the importance of treating and dealing with these mental health conditions because that way we can see why our current or future work (if we decide to work with this clinical population) is so important and hopefully rewarding.

Therefore, people with body dysmorphia avoid their normal activities that they used to like, they suffer from social, academic and work-related impairments, they remain single or discord in relationship, they become housebound and they become hospitalised.

Then there's the fact that people with body dysmorphia often try to commit suicide.

Therefore, whenever we question why body dysmorphia is important to look at, we need to investigate it and treat the condition to not only give someone back their life so they can start living again, but we need to save lives too.

<u>Cultural Variations In Body Dysmorphia</u>

In addition, to wrap up this introductory chapter on body dysmorphia, there are descriptions of the condition in series and case reports from a wide range of different countries. This is a "good" thing in the sense that it allows us to see patterns and although there are subtle differences between these reports in terms of client presentation, the clinical features are generally similar across cultures (Phillips, 1996).

The only downside to these results are that if a particular culture values appearance more strongly when compared to other cultures, then there is a chance this could predict higher rates of body dysmorphia, but that is a potential research gap. Since to empirically test that prediction we need good epidemiological surveys. Something we lack at the moment.

Yet the introductory information doesn't stop here for body dysmorphia because I wonder what are the different types of this condition and how do they differ?

MUSCLE DYSMORPHIA, DIAGNOSIS AND RISK FACTORS

Continuing our introduction to Body Dysmorphia, I want to introduce us to a small, subtype if you will of this particular mental health condition before exploring some risk factors and talking more about how Body Dysmorphia is diagnosed.

Muscle Dysmorphia

This type of Body Dysmorphia can be seen in one of the psychology article chapters about What's Wrong With The Perfect Body? Because this type of Body Dysmorphia is centred around a client believing that their body is too small or not muscular enough, so as you can imagine this is more common in men than women.

The other chapter explained the reasoning the reasoning behind it, but I need to mention it here because I want to keep all the Body Dysmorphia content together.

In addition, Muscle Dysmorphia makes a person very self-conscious about their muscles and body shape, leading to a preoccupation with muscle building and nutrition as well as this is associated with steroid abuse. Since steroids can help people build muscles but, of course, there are a lot of downsides including infertility.

Then if you've read a CBT book by me before then you know that any mental health condition has to be causing clinically significant levels of distress and is handicapping a person in their social life and job for them to be diagnosed.

Risk Factors

Similar to eating disorders, there are a range of risk factors that can increase the likelihood of someone developing and maintaining Body Dysmorphia. For example, if a person has low self-esteem and high perfectionism then this can cause them to want the "perfect body" and they develop Body Dysmorphia. Also, suffering childhood aversity and certain sociocultural values are risk factors too. These sociocultural values were addressed in another chapter about social media, the perfect body shape described by models and films and TV programmes, as well as what is deed to be the perfect body shape in your culture.

Furthermore, people can have genetic predisposition to Body Dysmorphia, that according to the Diathesis-Stress model these genetic vulnerabilities become expressed in response to environmental factors causing the condition to develop.

Another risk factor is being teased and bullied about their appearance, because this bullying can make the client self-conscious and focus more on their appearance and bullying decreases self-esteem to.

That's an important fact to mention how a person having one or two risk factors doesn't really impact them too much in the grand scheme of things depending on the severity and other life factors, but when a people has exposed to quite a number of risk factors without protective factors then this is when a person could be in trouble of developing Body Dysmorphia.

As well as it is arguable that all these risk factors increase a person's aesthetic sensitivity, so how sensitive they are to their looks being judged, criticized and commented on.

However, the biggest problem with Body Dysmorphia is that it is under-recognised and there is a low level of awareness within our communities and societies as a whole, but even more so for health practitioners.

The main reason for this is the client themselves, and I want to say up front here that I am flat out not blaming the client at all for their mental health condition. I know and I have spoken in many places that mental health conditions aren't the fault of the client, they are parts of people and whilst they can never be cured. We can give people more adaptive, safer and beneficial coping mechanisms so they can go on and live fairly clinically "normal" lives.

Similar to eating disorders, people with Body Dysmorphia don't tend to acknowledge they have a mental health difficulty and because of this they are very, very secretive. For example, they don't reveal their real symptoms unless they're asked, like you could think they have depression, OCD or social anxiety but you don't know why until they start revealing their concerns about their lack of muscles or the perfect body.

As well as people with Body Dysmorphia do present themselves to dermatologists or cosmetic surgeons, but again there is a lack of knowledge about this mental health condition, so hopefully this book can help raise awareness even slightly.

Furthermore, there is a lot of stigma surrounding Body Dysmorphia and even worse, people trivialise the condition. Due to surely it's okay for people to want to gain muscles and have the perfect body?

That might be true but if it starts negatively impacting their life, their job and their happiness then this does become a "problem" for the client and they need psychological help. As a result of this stigma and trivialisation, there is limited research on the condition and the lack of research and knowledge might lead to people with Body Dysmorphia getting misdiagnosed and treated with the wrong psychotherapy.

What Are The Screening Questions for Body Dysmorphia?

Something I love about clinical psychology, and you get to see this in the other CBT books as well, is that clinical psychologists are very clever at how they ask questions to get clients to reveal information they might never have revealed before, even to themselves.

There are some screening questions that are typically asked of people with suspected (at this stage) Body Dysmorphia.

- Some people are very bothered by the way they look. Is this a problem for you?
- How much does it bother you? What effect does it have on your life?
- What concerns you about your appearance?
- Does it make it hard to do your work or be with friends?
- How often do you think about it?
- On a typical day, in all how much do you think about it?
- How many hours a day?

Personally, I do like learning about screening questions because when it comes to mental health conditions and the faulty thinking patterns associated with them, a lot of maladaptive coping mechanisms and mental health difficulties aren't always clear to the clients. Therefore, by asking screening questions, we can start to understand what they're experiencing and we can start to think about how to help them before a "real" clinical assessment interview takes place.

But remember how I mentioned a moment ago that there is a chance of misdiagnosis in Body Dysmorphia cases, I wonder what these other diagnoses could be?

WHAT ABOUT DIFFERENTIAL DIAGNOSIS IN BODY DYSMORPHIA DISORDER?

This next chapter is definitely a good one because we deal with three different issues when it comes to clinical psychology and this is something we need to realise and deal with as future or current psychologists. We need to realise that just because it looks and acts like Body Dysmorphia, doesn't mean it is that condition, it could be another one.

Another problem is that the client might actually have Body Dysmorphia but is misdiagnosed as another condition and sometimes a client will have Body Dysmorphia and another mental health condition on top of that.

That is certainly something that makes clinical psychology fun and that is why I am so passionate about this brilliant subfield because there is much to learn, and so much to think about.

Differential Diagnosis: Eating Disorders

We know that Body Dysmorphia is about the preoccupation of having the perfect body but it's critical to remember that if a client's preoccupation is mainly focused on their perception of being too overweight. Then this is not Body Dysmorphia.

Instead this is an eating disorder because this client would lack the focus and obsessive with the body shape aspects of Body Dysmorphia, as they focus too much on weight side of things.

Instead when a client has an eating disorder and a comorbidity of Body Dysmorphia then they will have an excessive preoccupation with their shape and weight together, in addition to the other clinical features associated with both conditions.

Overall, there is an overlap in "disordered eating" and exercise dependence and/ or muscle dysmorphia.

Depression

Another tragic comorbidity common with Body Dysmorphia is depression, and the reason why I call this tragic is because people with Body Dysmorphia are often disgusted with themselves, have high levels of internal shame and they feel hopeless about alternating their appearance.

The depression typically develops after the Body Dysmorphia has already developed and can sometimes occur in recurrent depression, with the "magic wand" question typically being used by asking clients to imagine they have just woken up and all their problems are solved. They would be asked what has changed, how would they notice that their problems are gone and what would it make them feel.

Moreover, because depression is involved here and the clients feel hopeless about changing their appearance, it is critical that suicide risk is assessed. It is that sense of hopelessness that can unfortunately make people feel that suicide is the only way out of a bad situation.

That's why getting psychological help, support and guidance in the form of therapy is so critical for all mental health conditions but especially when depression is involved.

Social Phobia

Social Phobia or to name it more commonly Social Anxiety Disorder is common in people with body dysmorphia because both conditions share external shame and social anxiety as clinical features.

That's why when it comes to assessing people for body dysmorphia or social phobia, psychologists ask and explore the magic wand question, as well as "Guarantee not rating appearance" or "Desert Island" question.

Now I think these desert island questions are really fun in therapy, or they sound that way anyway, because not only are these light-hearted questions that therapists can ask to get information, but they help the client to reflect on what they cannot live without if they were ever stuck on a desert island.

In addition, social phobia is only ever comorbid

with body dysmorphia if the social fears the client has leads to humiliation or embarrassment, because that is a critical feature of social anxiety disorder. As well as if there is a co-morbid social phobia then this normally develops about 10 years before the body dysmorphia.

Therefore, as you can see after the first three other diagnoses, clinical psychology might not be straightforward but it is a lot of fun and it is fascinating, because you need to work out what condition the client has before working out how to help them.

Obsessive-Compulsive Disorder

OCD is another mental health condition that can happen alongside body dysmorphia since co-morbid OCD happens when the client has compulsions or obsessions that aren't restricted to concerns about appearance. They could have concerns about cleanliness or dirt as well.

As a result, OCD and body dysmorphia overlap when the client has fears about contamination on the associated with compulsive washing or psychogenic excoriation, and these thoughts and compulsions normally relate to order as well as symmetry. For instance, the client might believe that their hair has to feel exactly right and being exactly symmetrical.

Also, whilst the connection between contamination of skin and body dysmorphia might not appear clear just yet, this is important for the future chapters when we talk about skin picking and some of the extreme measures people with body dysmorphia take to "improve" their appearance.

Another Axis 1 Or Adjustment Disorder

Our final other diagnosis that we'll look at in the chapter might be one of the most heart-breaking in a way because unfortunate victims of moderate to severe burns, acne, alopecia and eczema do develop a mental health condition. Since if a person is preoccupied with a moderate to severe physical anomaly that is causing them psychological distress that and/ or impairs on their job, social and other areas of functioning then these people could have an adjustment disorder.

But that alone doesn't mean they have body dysmorphia.

For the client to have another condition and body dysmorphia together then they would have to see their body and body shake as the perceived defect too. If the person doesn't see their body shape as their defect then a diagnosis of Adjustment disorder or another diagnosis, like depression, might be given.

The cognitive models and risk factors for adjustment disorder and body dysmorphia are very similar in the sense that they both look at the role of teasing, and they both have similar therapeutic approaches with an additional therapy module that focuses on how to deal with teasing.

Furthermore, when a survey of body dysmorphia clients was done in specialist clinics (Veale 1996;

Phillips, 1993), the researchers found that the mean age of onset in adolescence was 16 years old but the mean age of assessment was 31 years old with there being an equal sex ratio for clients. As well as two-thirds of clients were single or separated and it wasn't uncommon for them to have a co-morbidity condition, like social phobia, OCD or depression, as well as a high suicide risk. Also, a co-morbid personality disorder or to use more modern terminology Complex Emotional Needs wasn't uncommon either.

Overall, I wanted to mention these findings to really hammer home the importance of this chapter and not believing that a person can only ever have a single mental health condition at any one time. It's important to treat all the conditions that a person has and whilst this makes it more complex, difficult and tricky for a psychologist to do, it certainly doesn't make our current or future jobs boring.

And it makes them a lot more rewarding too if we're successful.

CHILD AND ADOLESCENTS WITH BODY DYSMORPHIA, CLINICAL FEATURES AND BIASED COGNITIVE PROCESSES

Before we start talking about treatment options and cognitive models used to explain body dysmorphia, we need to explore the difference between adults and children having the condition, the clinical features of body dysmorphia as well as how this condition leads to biased cognitive processes compared to clinically normal people.

This is definitely an interesting chapter.

<u>Children & Adolescents With Body Dysmorphia</u>

Personally, I always find it a bit difficult to talk about children and teenagers with mental health difficulties because at heart, I suppose I always want to imagine children being happy, enjoying life and never ever struggling. Granted I've written entire books based on the mental health difficulties of children and adolescents but I suppose me becoming an uncle four days before I write this made me a little more cautious.

Anyway, when it comes to body dysmorphia the clinical presentation of children is similar to adults but there is a more of a continuum when compared to normal adolescence. Due to in a way every teenager I know compares and hates their body shape and weight during these times, but again, it is the psychological distress and significant impairment in areas of functioning that gets a child a diagnosis.

In addition, when compared to adults, adolescents with body dysmorphia have a higher lifetime suicide rate as well as their beliefs are more delusional (Phillips, 2006). Therefore, children with body dysmorphia are more likely to experience social isolation, stop partaking in sport, refuse to go to school and have conflict with family members. Yet there is no data on prevalence unfortunately.

Another source used here is Mataix-Cols et al. (2015).

What Are The Clinical Features?

In the past few chapters, we have focused on this somewhat but there are a lot of different areas of a client's behaviour that is impacted by body dysmorphia, and whilst some of this information is repeated through a different lens in later chapters, it's really important to have all this information upfront.

As a result, I hinted at earlier that body dysmorphia is all about a person having a preoccupation with their body weight and shape, but this preoccupation shows in other ways as well. For example, the preoccupation makes the features of concern painfully embarrassing for the client so much so that it causes their high levels of psychological distress.

In addition, the preoccupation is difficult to control or resist because the client ruminates on their appearance, it is time-consuming and it makes a client have ideas or delusions about their body weight and shape.

Moreover, clients with body dysmorphia think it is too hard for them to problem solve and they often identify the wrong "problem" to solve. For example, they would want to solve the problem of the shape of their nose when in reality, they need to solve the "problem" of their biased cognitive processes that makes their nose the problem.

Due to the cycle a client with body dysmorphia tends to go through is:

- Ruminate on unsolvable "problem"- like "why am I so ugly?" and "If only I could fix my nose?"
- Worry and create social anxiety for themselves based on non-existent problems in the future. Like "Oh if someone says something about my nose I'll want the ground to swallow me up and kill me,"
- Judging, self-blame, self-attacking and punish themselves.

- Compare their features to others.
- Plan to alter the feature of concern

This process is what therapy aims to change.

Yet until that time a client still has the massive preoccupation.

Leading to a client hoping to rectify or "save" themselves from the perceived threat of other people seeing the feature of concern in the form of safety behaviours, something we focus more on later. These safety behaviours include:

- Mirror Gazing
- Camouflaging (trying to hid the area of concern)
- Repeated Checking Of Body Part
- Skin Cleaning, Picking, Peeling, Bleaching
- Ritualized Or Excessive Make-Up
- Reassurance Seeking
- Grooming, Combing, Smoothening, Straightening, Plucking Or Cutting Hair
- Comparing Self With Others Or Old Photos
- Facial Exercises
- Excessive Use Of Hair & Beauty Products

I know that was a brief look at safety behaviours but that's because we look at them in a later chapter in more applied ways as well as discussing why these are so critical to understand in Cognitive Behavioural

Therapy. And I do love learning and talking about safety behaviours too.

Social Anxiety

Building upon what we learnt in the last chapter about the social anxiety that body dysmorphia causes because of the fear the client has over their features of concern and the associated negative evaluation they are fearful of getting (Phillips et al., 1993; Veale et al., 1996; Hollander and Aronowitz, 1999; Pinto and Phillips, 2005; Coles et al., 2006; Anson et al. 2012), there is something I want to add here.

Due to whilst the job of a psychologist in terms of diagnosis is to get the mental health condition right for the client and this involves a hell of a lot of elimination work, the entire reason why a person should be diagnosed with body dysmorphia and not social phobia or another anxiety disorder is two-fold.

Firstly, the client with body dysmorphia has a preoccupation with their body shape and weight, this is not a clinical feature of social phobia.

Secondly, whilst there is overlap between the two conditions, a psychologist would always select the diagnosis that BEST explains what the client is experiencing, and when you add in the clinical features of body dysmorphia, it becomes clear that only a body dysmorphia diagnosis explains what a client is experiencing.

Can a client have body dysmorphia and social phobia?

Of course they can because body dysmorphia

clients can receive an additional diagnosis of social phobia if they experience significant anxiety related to negative evaluation of social characteristics or behaviours.

Then again not everyone with body dysmorphia gets really bad (significant) anxiety in social situations.

<u>Appearance Comparison</u>

In addition, something I find really interesting is appearance comparison, because we all do it and I talk about the self-esteem reasons why we do this in <u>Social Psychology</u>. Yet clients with body dysmorphia compare their body shape and weight to other people, especially with members of the same sex, in a wide range of social situations. Like public or social situations, on social media or when viewing other forms of media representations. Similar to eating disorders in that sense.

This appearance comparison of is one of the most frequently reported symptoms in BDD (Anson et al., 2015; Phillips et al., 1993; 1995; Phillips, 1996).

<u>Compulsive skin-picking</u>

This is definitely a major part of body dysmorphia that I've been looking forward to talking about, because this involves repetitive skin-picking and cleaning, especially of the face with the aim of this behaviour being to remove blemishes, scabs, moles and freckles. As you can probably imagine this is damaging, it can scar a person and it can cause them a lot of pain.

And even more heartbreaking and I'll admit I am getting uncomfortable just writing this paragraph, but to do these they use fingernails, tweezers, pins, sharp implements.

Naturally this leads to bleeding, bruises, infections as well as (or occasionally) permanent disfigurement.

Overall, this is a strategy that results in short term tension in the client being reduced and them having high satisfaction only followed by disgust, anger and depression.

Attentional Processes In Body Dysmorphia

Like all mental health conditions, body dysmorphia causes a person's cognitive processes to become biased and that is the entire basis of the cognitive approach too. One of these biased processes in body dysmorphia is an attentional bias because when a client looks in a mirror, they have a bias towards specific features compared to overall appearance, like a spot on their left cheek, one ear being a little bigger than the other and they lack a self-serving bias. Think of this has seeing yourself through "rose tinted glasses").

Resulting in an increased aesthetic sensitivity for their feature and emotional bias.

Attitudes About Appearance

Then these attentional biases leads a client developing negative attitudes about their appearance and their so-called defect (whether these are real or imagined) with these attitudes being associated with increased distress and avoidance behaviours.

Some of these negative attitudes include a person self-objectifying as well as having an idealised value about the importance of their appearance.

Overall, to wrap up these first few chapters on what is body dysmorphia, you need to remember that with this condition everything is about appearance with the idea being that a client doesn't want to look stunning (but some will), they just want to fit in with other people. And because of one or more areas of concern, they don't believe they can do that.

As well as clients with the condition believe their appearance has to be perfect and they want to feel comfortable with their appearance before they can do anything else. This is why the impairment in social, job and other areas of functioning occurs.

With the most deep-seated belief being that they can never ever be satisfied with their appearance.

How can we start treating these people?

COGNITIVE MODELS OF BODY DYSMORPHIA

Now we understand what is Body Dysmorphia, the psychological features amongst other basic information surrounding the condition, we need to examine the cognitive models that aim to explain how it develops and maintains before we can ever hope to understand why Cognitive Behavioural Therapy is as effective as it is for this condition.

To understand the cognitive models we can look at research by Veale and Neziroglu (2010), Veale et al. (1996); Veale (2004), Wilhelm (2006), Buhlmann & Wilhelm (2004) and Rosen (1995).

<u>CBT Model and Formulation</u>

Veale et al. proposes that Body Dysmorphia develops because of a client's vulnerability to the condition, and they placed an emphasis on their appearance in the family and their own perfectionism. As well as their early life and past experiences, like bullying and teasing, and this leads to them having specific appearance concerns, evaluations and associated beliefs they have. For example, the client might argue that their nose is too large, that they're very unattractive or they value their attractiveness highly so much so that it is a core defining feature of their self.

Additionally, Veale et al. propose that a person's negative internal thoughts, impression and images as well as the associated distressing meaning or the feared consequences for the person interacts with the following features:

- Checking behaviours
- Attempts to correct body concerns
- Rumination and comparing
- Mood changes
- Avoidance and safety behaviours
- Self-focused attention
- Fear of negative evaluation

All those features lead to people having negative beliefs about themselves and their appearance, and the fascinating thing about this model is it looks at how everything interacts and plays into each other. For instance, if we take the classic example of safety behaviours, the short definition is these are behaviours a client does to feel safe about their thoughts and feelings otherwise they feel like they will die if they don't do them. Such as whenever a client with Body Dysmorphia gets a negative thought about their so-called pathetic shape, their safety behaviour might be to go to the gym immediately, have a protein shake or wear certain clothes that increases their appearance. If the client doesn't do these safety behaviours then they will belief something catastrophic will happen to them.

But of course these safety behaviours only maintain the beliefs about their importance so the safety behaviours get reinforced, lead to negative beliefs and this leads to the person having negative internal thoughts, impression and images all over again. Creating a clear cycle that therapy aims to break.

Maintaining Factors

If you've read any of the other CBT books then you would know how much I love maintaining factors because I find them fascinating and I like safety behaviours even more because they are the biggest cons that we pull on ourselves. Since safety behaviours are fully intended to protect us from threat or prevent harm coming to us. As a result, these safety behaviours might reduce our anxiety in the short term, but they always have the unintended consequence of maintaining anxiety in the longer term.

That's why I think safety behaviours are very interesting cons that we pull on ourselves because we convince ourselves that we're helping ourselves to be less anxious, and if we don't do these behaviours we're going to basically die. But in reality, they're making us "worse", not "better".

However, if we apply this knowledge to body dysmorphia then a person's safety and avoidance behaviours only reinforce their preoccupation with their appearance and self-focused attention, as well as their sense that their appearance is flawed.

Also, the biggest "danger" so to speak about safety behaviours is that they prevent people from disconfirming their beliefs about the feared events. For example, let's take a very stereotypical example of a man with body dysmorphia believing that without a six pack he will never meet the partner of his dreams and he will only be met with negative evaluations and comments by others, so he engages with safety behaviours. The problem with that is his safety behaviours don't allow him to test his theories about never being able to meet the partner of his dreams.

Because he will never put himself in that situation to meet someone, because in their eyes, what's the point of trying to find someone when my appearance is so pig ugly?

Another example of safety behaviours in action is if we focus on the social anxiety part of body dysmorphia, because in social and public situations, safety behaviours and the excessive self-focused attention that is common in body dysmorphia will likely interfere with the person's accurate observations of other people's reactions. For example, a woman at the party just smiles at the person because they believe the client is attractive, but the client might misread that as them making fun of them and their so-called pathetic appearance.

Overall, safety behaviours prevent the client from disconfirming any perceptions they have about negative evaluations of their appearance by others. As well as their safety behaviours and self-focused attention could "contaminate" their environment as well so their beliefs are confirmed.

And the easiest example of the latter is in social anxiety because if a client has a fear about people staring at them and they start staring at people to make sure they aren't being focused on. Then as you can imagine over time people will stare at the client because they're staring at them, so that only confirms the negative and biased beliefs they hold.

So after exploring a lot of the psychological theories and background information about body dysmorphia, how do we start treating the condition using Cognitive Behavioural Therapy?

STARTING THE CBT PROCESS FOR BODY DYSMORPHIA

In the section of the book where we spoke about CBT for eating disorders, we introduced a lot of basic information about Cognitive Behavioural Therapy so I'm not going to repeat that too much.

Since CBT assessments and treatments all run on a four stage system where a clinical assessment appears then there is engagement in alternative more adaptive coping mechanisms where as formulation is developed and then CBT for body dysmorphia includes specific modules tailored to this condition.

Now we're going to apply those four stages to body dysmorphia.

<u>Engagement In The First Session</u>

In the first chapter on body dysmorphia I mentioned that clients can become housebound and be socially impaired, thankfully CBT can be very flexible about the location depending on what's required. Since it can happen in a therapy office, over the phone, a home visit or even a car park.

Then of course, during the therapy process it is critical not to trivialise the client's symptoms or shame the person for being vain. Due to a psychologist has to appear knowledgeable and be credible.

In addition, in the first session, you explore what the agenda of the therapy process is for the client and what are their expectations. The last thing you want is for them to think everything is a quick fix and they'll be cured and never ever have these concerns again after a few sessions.

That really isn't how therapy works.

Therefore, some psychologists help these questions:

- "What would you hope for by the end of our consultation"
- "How do you feel about seeing me?"
- "Why have you sought help now?"

Furthermore, in the first session, a psychologist would need to assess the client's ambivalence. This is generally about finding if the client has come to you out of their own freewill or because they've been pressured by someone. This could be a medical doctor, a parent, a friend or a cosmetic surgeon or dermatologist.

Ideally the client would always come to you freely because that signals they could have the engagement needed to complete the therapy successfully, but not everyone is like that and even a pressured person can become engaged over time and complete the therapy successfully.

As well as the therapist will conduct an of the preoccupation the person has. Normally asking "On an average day, how many minutes or hour(s) do you currently spend thinking about your features? Please add up all the time that your features are at the forefront of your mind and make the best estimate."

The general consensus is that if it's over one hour a day then they probably do have body dysmorphia and they need therapy because that is a lot of time. It is even more time when you consider that a person would ideally only be awake for 16 hours of the day instead of the 24 hours.

Assessment Of Perceived "Defect"

Another job of a psychologist during the first session is to assess the extent of the client's perceptions surrounding their "defect". Of course the purpose of this is two-fold. Firstly, you want to know how severe the perception is ranging from good insights that is only slightly "wrong" compared to reality all the way up to delusional beliefs. Secondly, a psychologist needs to know if there actually is a defect.

The second point is important because a client might be referred to them under pressure because of others' perception about the client. When it turns out in reality, the client has every right to be concerned about the "defect".

For example, if we go back to our burn victim example from earlier, if a client keeps becoming concerned with their burn marks on their face and the people surrounding the client believe they have nothing to worry about or they're being delusional about the severity of the burn marks. Then the client might come to a psychologist because the client believes they are being delusional, when in reality they aren't.

As a result, a psychologist might ask: *can you tell me what specific concerns do you have about your appearance?*

In this case, the client needs to tell the psychologist about the feature that they perceive as flawed or defective, and most importantly why. The feature could be too big, small, asymmetrical or disproportionate to the rest of the face or body. Thinning hair, acne, scars, wrinkles, vascular markings, being too pale or ruddy in complexion or even not muscular enough are all examples are that.

Sometimes, these can be very vague or a general perception of them being ugly, "not right" or too masculine or feminine.

Although at times, there are likely to be multiple locations, normally on the face, that are the perceived defects. Also, psychologists typically use a pie chart to show how to visually work with the client to identify any similarities between the concerns and perceived defects. One oversimplified example would be if a client has a too small left ear, nose and lips. That could be shown to the client easily and CBT is one of the more visual therapies.

Also, these features of concern can and do fluctuate over time and shift to other areas. As well as a person can admit and accept that they look normal to other people but they feel abnormal.

That's why when it comes to assessing the "perceived defect", a psychologist typically asks about:

- How ugly/ unattractive he/she thinks the feature is?
- How noticeable or abnormal it is without camouflage (like make-up)?

Interestingly, at times these features discussed in body dysmorphia might have actually changed for the worse and this is real, like after a cosmetic surgery, or the features have changed for a reason they can't explain easily, like after a drug experience.

Leading us onto our next section.

Examination Of Feature or Features of Concern

So how does a psychologist see if these concerns are based in reality or not?

As a result, a psychologist would need to ask permission to see these features up close, and sometimes this does require clients removing clothing (just not anything inappropriate though) or taking off make-up.

If a psychologist can't view the feature because the client refuses to move the make-up or it's inappropriate, then this is a tough one, a really tough one. Due to without seeing the feature or features for themselves, a psychologist just can't make a great judgement about how noticeable or abnormal the feature really is.

In this case then they NEED corroborative evidence from a relative or doctor.

Overall, the entire point of this part of the first session is to find out the extent of the discrepancy between the client's self-rating or self-portrait and therapist's rating of the noticeability or abnormality and discrepancy with the client's ideal self. As well as some features might be "noticeable" but still be within normal human variation and might be easily satisfied by surgery.

<u>Observation</u>

As you might know from reading other clinical psychology books or attending lectures, observations and watching our clients is an extremely powerful tool within our profession. Therefore, when it comes to body dysmorphia the client's looks can give us clues about the condition.

For example, it would be useful to notice the following:

- Is the client wearing a hat, baseball cap, sunglasses, baggy clothes, scarf?
- Does the person find it difficult to make eye contact?
- Is the person sitting in particular way to hide the worst side?

- Is the person heavily made up?
- Does the person have long hair to hide their face?
- Are there are scars from skin-picking?

All of these are important to note because they help to provide the psychologist with good information about how the client perceives their "defects" and how others will perceive them in turn.

In addition, a psychologist should always ask about the motivation behind these behaviours, like the excessive make up and skin picking, because if these behaviours are related to body dysmorphia then these can all be added to the list of safety behaviours the client shows.

Distress and impact

Lastly, for this chapter, a therapist or psychologist would need to make a clinical judgement on the degree of the client's distress as well as how this interferes with the client's social life, home and family relationships, their dating and intimacy and their ability to study or work.

It's all important for the diagnosis.

After getting all this information then the psychologist could make a diagnosis and they can explain what body dysmorphia means to the client.

Also, it is flat out critical that the psychologist does not under any circumstances explain the condition as an "imagined defect" but instead a "preoccupation and severe distress with the way you feel about your appearance" or "difference between the way you feel about your appearance and what others say".

That is a much kinder way to talk about them and their beliefs. You never want to invalidate someone in therapy, or life to be honest.

In addition, psychologists should never say to a client that they have a "distorted" perception because that's not validating. Instead they should try something like, they've lost rose-tinted glasses and "better at judging aesthetics" and "body image has become mixed with feelings of disgust/ shame".

Moreover, they shouldn't argue about the diagnosis because the psychologist should be validating the client's distress and handicap and encourage them to test out alternative theories, which is something we cover later on and that's the entire point of CBT anyway.

However, psychologists do need to be careful with terms like "acceptance" or "coping" because it's very disheartening if the client interprets those terms as resigning themselves to be ugly forever. That's why some psychologists say something along the lines of "body image is not just a photo on the back of your eye. It depends on feelings, how self-focused you are and ghosts from the past".

That's a much kinder way to explain what's going on for clients and that simple act of kindness is extremely powerful not only for the client themselves, but the therapeutic alliance too.

MORE ON CBT FOR BODY DYSMORPHIA

To further explore what was discussed in the last chapter, in this chapter, we're going to talk a little about the different psychometric measures that are used in body dysmorphia cases and then we'll explore engagement a little more.

Including a very interesting way to frame engagement.

Yale Brown Obsessive Compulsive Scale Modified for Body Dysmorphia

This model was created by Phillips et al. (1997) and it provides an objective observer a standardised way to rate the outcome measures. These outcome measures are thinking and activity for time occupied, distress, resistance, and control are measured plus 2 items on insight and avoidance. This is a 12-item survey.

In addition, the scores for this survey range from 0 to 48 and for access into a clinical trial or psychological treatment a score greater than 22 is required. As well as any score higher than 36 is needed to meet the severe criteria for body dysmorphia.

Appearance Anxiety Inventory

Furthermore, considering the psychological distress and anxiety involved in body dysmorphia, an anxiety inventory is needed. As a result the AAI was created by Veale et al. (2014) and this is used to measure weekly progress, so this psychometric measure is a little different from other ones we've looked at before.

Also, whilst this inventory has 10 items scored according to their frequency, in reality this is an inventory made up of two subscales. The first is about avoidance behaviours made up of 6 items, and the second is about threat monitoring with 4 items. As well as on the inventory scores range from 0 to 40.

Engagement

Now I did want to circle back to engagement because it is so critical in all psychological therapies, but even more so for body dysmorphia.

Therefore, this mixes in with clinical formulation because formulations are idiosyncratic versions of psychological models because they are tailored to the individual so a psychologist knows what exactly is maintaining the distress and preoccupation within a person. This is a lot better for our clients compared to formulations to get them involved and to some extent when a formulation is done they have no choice but to get engaged and involved to some extent.

So there is some natural engagement building in formulations.

On the other hand, there is the two theory technique to build engagement. Since you get the client to compare Theory A (this is everywhere they're been doing so far like their maladaptive coping mechanisms, safety behaviours and biased cognitive processes). This is the theory that you're trying to challenge and change because it's led them to become handicapped.

Then you have Theory B which is an emotional problem that makes the client excessively self-conscious about their appearance. For example, their experiences of bullying.

Afterward a psychologist has outlined the theories, they might ask a client:

- Have you noticed that solving the "problem" as an appearance problem makes your preoccupation and distress worse?
- Have you tried to deal with your problem as if it was Theory "B"?.......
- Would you be prepared to act as if it was Theory "B" for at least three months?

Then it is about working with the client to see how they might want to work with the Theory B idea because these two theories are exclusive of each other, and it's about opening the client's mind to other possible alternatives that will be built on later in the therapy.

COGNITIVE BEHAVIOURAL ASSESSMENT

This next chapter builds on what I spoke about in the chapter introducing treatment options for eating disorders, because this chapter focuses on cognitive behaviour assessments from a body dysmorphia standpoint. There are a lot of differences between the assessment for both types of mental health conditions, but it's still really interesting to see the similarities as well.

Therefore, when it comes to body dysmorphia, an assessment is about starting to build an alternative understanding of both the developmental and maintaining factors of the condition.

Onset Of Body Dysmorphia

That's why looking at the onset of body dysmorphia in a person is important, because it allows a psychologist to understand the developmental factors behind the condition.

Therefore, the client reveals the earliest point

they remember having significant appearance concerns, what features of their body they're concerned about and what their general feelings are about their appearance when they were a child and in adolescence.

This helps psychologists to understand how the condition developed over time, and this is made even clearer when the client reveals what are the specific events or triggers associated with the development of these body shape and weight concerns. These could be bullying events about their appearance, any perceived changes in appearance or any cosmetic procedures the client had done.

Furthermore, in a clinical assessment, the psychologist might get the client to link imagery to their past experiences and this is a way to check how accurate or biased their cognitive processes are. For example, a psychologist could ask something along the lines of *How old were you when you first experienced the image?*, basically asking the client about a "ghost from their past". Then using this information, the psychologist can explore what was happening in their client's life at that time, what were the client's beliefs at the time and if those beliefs and the meaning the client gave to that event still feel relevant today.

Maintenance factors

When it comes to clinical assessments, finding out what the maintaining factors are are flat out critical because a mental health condition cannot exist without them. That's why it is important for psychologists to discover them and these maintaining factors come out of two places. Avoidance and safety-seeking behaviours as well as Cognitive processes.

Both of these categories have a critical function for the client because they either help them to monitor or reduce the perceived threat and they provide experiential avoidance for the client.

These maintaining factors can be further complicated for an assessment by a depressed mood. Since you don't know the role of the depressed mood for the body dysmorphia.

In terms of avoidance behaviour, these can be specific. For example, a client hates their body dysmorphia or gets "worse" in medical examination sports, swimming, public changing rooms, when being intimate, in certain clothes or lighting, around others when taking a photo, in mirrors or reflective surfaces, being physically close to others or in certain haircuts.

In this situation, then the client can live a fairly clinically normal life because they can simply avoid these places and function in other places.

However, avoidance behaviours can be general too meaning their body dysmorphia "flares up" in a wide range of social and public situations resulting in the client coming housebound.

As a result, in a clinical assessment, a psychologist would need to understand the frequency of these avoidance behaviours, as well as the motivation. Since they need to know if the behaviour is fear-driven, designed to prevent a lengthy compulsion or because of low motivation. To assess this the question of *what would you predict would happen if you were to do x?* could be used to find a psychologist a starting point.

<u>Safety Seeking Behaviours</u>

Moreover, when it comes to safety behaviours these need to be assessed in therapy too so the psychologist knows what they need to help the client unlearn. Due to these behaviours are done to avoid a threat, like taking away other the person's attention from the feature of concern, and this needs to be constantly monitored or verified against the mental image of their ideal self.

However, these safety behaviours are problematic because of the unintended consequences it has for a client's increased awareness, distress and preoccupation.

As a result, a psychologist needs to assess the motivation behind these safety behaviours, like it could be the client hopes they look different or they're mentally preparing themselves for the worst or to reduce the threat.

Some examples of these safety behaviours can be seen in different areas of a client's life. For example, if a client is in public then they would have social anxiety resulting in them making poor eye contact, keeping their head down, comparing themselves to others, changing their posture and hiding the feature of concern behind their hand.

Whereas when they're in private, the client would be checking in mirrors, in reflective surfaces or directly, checking with their fingers, taking photos, using make-up, comparing against others on social media, seeking confirmation of their concerns and skin-picking.

For the purposes of a clinical assessment, the client would have to monitor the frequency of these behaviours and if the count is high then it might be best for them to use a tally.

Cognitive Processes

Building upon what we spoke about earlier, in a clinical assessment, a psychologist would need to look at a client's cognitive processes because if they have a mental health condition then these will be biased in different ways depending on the condition.

When it comes to body dysmorphia, a client's perceptual processes will be biased, including their attentional bias and their increased self-focused attention. It is these biased processes that make them so focus on their appearance.

Therefore, in a clinical interview, it's important to identify with the client any motivations or beliefs they have about their cognitive processes by engaging in metacognition (thinking about thinking) as well as conduct a functional analysis on their perseverative processes and avoidant or excessive behaviours.

Cosmetic Procedures

One aspect of body dysmorphia we haven't addressed yet is cosmetic procedures, because with clients hating their appearance and wanting to fix their areas of concern, they would have thought about or even tried to have a cosmetic or dermatological procedure.

Then the success of this procedure will have an effect on the preoccupation and distress. Since clients tend to feel anger, guilt or regret towards the surgeon because the procedure might help them for a while but ultimately they will always find a feature to be concerned about because of their biased cognitive processes.

Equally if a client hasn't had a procedure yet then it's important to understand what's stopping them and how serious is their plan for "improving" their feature of concern.

And ideally everyone would, but it's important for a psychologist to try to encourage the client to engage in Cognitive Behavioural Therapy before considering a procedure.

Interestingly, if the client has very serious plans for a cosmetic procedure, it is normally recommended to delay CBT until a few months after any procedure. Mainly because you can't stop the person from dreaming of surgery.

Also, it's important to show flexibility because that can help boost engagement later on because if you're willing to be kind, good and supportive then the client will remember and respect that. Then normally follow-up appointments are offered for after the procedure too.

Personally, I found that surprising to find out because I would have imagined you would encourage them to have therapy *before* the procedure so they could hopefully cancel it, save themselves money and not risk making their concern of feature "worse" in their eyes or make it actually worse because of a bad procedure.

Yet it does make complete sense because you really cannot stop people if they really want something.

Speaking of a quick note on engagement, a client's current solutions are unworkable because of the disruption, distress and impairment in areas of functioning they cause clients, so the aim of psychological therapy is to give the psychologist and client a good psychological understanding of what is maintaining their distress and preoccupation, because the client being told they look "alright" is useless.

Then therapy for body dysmorphia involves, on average, 16 sessions, but it could be as long as 20 to 30 sessions.

Goals In Therapy

The final topic we need to talk about in this chapter is certainly a firm favourite of mine and that is goal setting in psychotherapy. Now if you want to explore my own thoughts and see why psychometric and personal goals are beyond critical in therapy then please check out my book, *Clinical Psychology Reflections Volume 4*.

However, when it comes to goal setting in therapy for body dysmorphia, a core part of engagement and motivation is working with the client to create short-, medium- and long term goals. These are normally psychometric in nature, for example, let's aim to reduce your AAI score by ten points. But they are personal as well.

This gives the client something they want to work towards and this helps them to get more invested in the process.

To do this, psychologists and clients work together to find goals that they can both agree on. For instance, to decrease their preoccupation and their distress over appearance, or to stop skin-picking. Those would be medium-term goals.

Whereas short term goals could be to decrease their self-focused attention, decrease the number of times they compare themselves to others, or mirror gazing and other safety behaviours. Also, longer term goals are linked to the client's values, like decreasing the sheer importance the client places on their appearance.

Yet this all raises a very interesting question, what techniques and interventions could a psychologist use to change and challenge the biased cognitive processes we've spoken about?

COGNITIVE INTERVENTIONS FOR BODY DYSMORPHIA

Everything so far in the body dysmorphia section of the book has been leading to this single chapter in all fairness, because now we're going to focus on what interventions or techniques are used within cognitive behavioural therapy to help change and challenge a client's biased cognitive processes, safety behaviours and avoidance behaviours.

Since the point of CBT is to help a client reduce their unhelpful cognitive processes and behaviours. Including:

- Excessive checking of the features of concern be it in mirrors, reflective surfaces, touching or photos.
- Excessive avoidance of seeing their body
- Zooming in /selective attention bias
- Excessive comparing to others
- Safety behaviours

- Excessive grooming and preparation
- Negative interpretations of reactions of others
- Reassurance seeking
- Excessive self-focused attention
- Avoidance of social and public situations and photos.

CBT aims to deal with all of these aspects.

Dealing With Appearance Comparison

One of the aspects a psychologist helps the client deal with in therapy is their appearance comparison. During therapy, a psychologist would help the client to be aware of the times when they compare or scrutinise their appearance compared to others.

The strategies used here are aimed at helping the client to resist or disengage from these comparing behaviours by shifting their attention from the person they're comparing themselves with to other aspects of the environment or situation.

Target Rumination

I've mentioned a number of times during the last two sections about how body dysmorphia leads to rumination. Therefore, we absolutely have to target this in therapy, which is why we'll look at what Watkins, Wells, Linehan and Gilbert have proposed.

Due to these researchers propose in therapy, a client needs to identify times when they are ruminating, comparing or self-attacking. Then they need to determine the supporting meta-cognitions of the process. For example, they could realise that ruminating is stopping them from thinking they look okay or it is mentally preparing them for being humiliated. Once this is realised these meta-cognitions can be questioned pragmatically by getting the client to focus on their cost and inconsistency with Theory B.

Afterwards, the client can do a functional analysis on the process of ruminating so they can understand what function is the ruminating trying to fulfil in that particular context, what is the response and what are its consequences. And it is when the client starts to realise the negative impact that these behaviours are having on themselves that real change starts to occur.

In addition, the client should identify the self-focused attention and the therapy helps them to re-attend the external world. In a way by practising detached mindfulness so instead of focusing on your thoughts and your actions, you need to focus on the surroundings and stop focusing on yourself.

Finally, the client should turn "why" into "how" because if they ask "why" then they aren't focused on changing their rumination and changing their life for the better. "Why" gets them to keep focusing on themselves when we need them to focus on other things like, "how" are they going to do the things that they value in their life and stop avoiding them?

Mirror Retraining

By this point in the book, you might have gotten the idea that mirrors are one of the worse things for people with body dysmorphia and this feeds into their maladaptive relationship with their body shape and weight. Therefore, in therapy, a client needs to be retrained in their relationship with mirrors.

This starts with the client identifying the motivation for why they look at mirrors and they agree with the psychologist a criteria for termination, as well as goals for agreed function.

Afterwards, a client could use a large mirror at a slight distance and stand there in a non-judgemental way with minimal or no make-up. Due to the problem here is that the client believes they look awful, disgusting and ugly so if we get them to realise on their own that they actually aren't then this is very helpful.

As a result, we get the client to focus their attention on their external reflection and get them to look at their whole body or face without focusing on their feature of concern, using a range of lights and mirrors.

Of course, none of these mirrors are magnifying because we don't want the client to think they need to focus on any part of them. As well as ambiguous surfaces aren't used either.

The entire point of this exercise is to show the client they are okay as they are, they don't need to focus on any part of their body because they look great as they are and nothing bad will happen to them if they don't engage in safety behaviours.

Speaking of which.

Target Safety Seeking Behaviours

Whilst I'll deal with safety behaviours quickly because they are dealt with probably in the next chapter using my all-time favourite psychological technique, behavioural experiments, I need to address briefly about cognitive interventions are used to deal with safety behaviours.

We know from previous chapters that safety behaviours are triggered in private, public and social situations so exposure or behavioural experiments are used to give a client controlled exposure to a situation they avoid without using their safety behaviours, with the therapist aiding them at the beginning.

Also, predictions are made by the client before the experiment begins and then these are reviewed afterwards. I include a great example in the next chapter.

When it comes to body dysmorphia some examples include:

- Going outdoors and bright lighting- perfect for housebound clients
- Walk around a shopping centre
- Go shopping for clothes
- Having a haircut
- Classroom environment
- Changing room at a swimming pool or something.

These are all about showing clients that nothing

bad will happen and they aren't going to die if they don't use their safety behaviours, and 99.99% of the time they are far, far better off without their maladaptive safety behaviours.

How Cognitive Behaviour Deals With Social Situations?

Building upon this further, CBT for body dysmorphia gets a client to work with a psychologist to create an exposure hierarchy or behavioural experiments (with or without safety behaviour but more on this later) to help show them how their safety behaviours impact their self-consciousness, frequency of thoughts and disconfirm fears of negative evaluation.

Therefore, cognitive interventions are used to help deal with social situations and social anxiety similar to how exposure therapy is used to treat anxiety disorders. Since these help people to enter anxiety-provoking situations and drop safety behaviours.

Cognitive Interventions For Skin-Picking and Hair Cutting

With skin-picking and hair cutting being serious and costly safety behaviours in body dysmorphia, these do require addressing in CBT. This is done through work with the client that gets them to conduct a detailed functional analysis of the behaviour so they know exactly what the causes and consequences are of the behaviour, allowing them to see the damage it is doing to them and those around them.

In addition, this means the client needs to monitor themselves and what triggers this skin-picking behaviour, reverse the habit they've developed and in therapy, they need to find an alternative stimulation for their fingers. For example, normally when the clients gets triggered they pick their skin, but in therapy they need to find something else to do with their fingers, like tapping or something that isn't harmful.

Furthermore, the client's beliefs about skin-picking would be challenged too in therapy but the big problem with this maladaptive behaviour is that clients skin-picking because it causes very short term satisfaction. And that is very difficult to treat and replace because it makes the client feel good.

So how could behavioural experiments further help clients with body dysmorphia?

CBT FOR EATING DISORDERS AND BODY DYSMORPHIC DISORDER

BEHAVIOURAL EXPERIMENTS IN BODY DYSMORPHIA

Long time readers of mine will know that I personally love behavioural experiments, they are amazing and they are such a powerful tool for a therapist to use that I cannot recommend learning about them enough. They are really important and fun to know.

Therefore, my intention for this chapter is to mention the beliefs involved in body dysmorphia again because these are the beliefs that need to be tested using behavioural experiments. Then I'll explain what these brilliant tools are before applying this to body dysmorphia at the end.

Beliefs About Appearance

By the time the therapy process moves onto even thinking about behavioural experiments, they would have felt that the client is ready to identify and question their evaluations and values associated with their appearance. These include their overly negative evaluation of their appearance, the excessive importance they attach to appearance, as well as the excessive importance their appearance is in defining the self as a whole.

Then since this is cognitive behavioural therapy after all, the client's views about the self, others and the world are challenged too. This is everything that behavioural experiments aim to challenge and help a client to change.

Behavioural Experiments

I absolutely love because Behavioural Experiments are so cool, amazing and just flat out brilliant. I love learning about them and if you ever find a good video of these being done properly or you get to use them or see them in real life, you'll realise how amazing they are too.

However, for the sake of clarity, a behavioural experiment is:

"Planned experiential activities, based on experimentation or observation, which are undertaken by clients in or between sessions" (Bennett-Levy, J., Butler, G. Fennell, M., Hackmann, A., Mueller, M. & Westbrook, D., 2004).

As well as these are very powerful to combating safety behaviours and their design is directly generated from cognitive formulations of presenting problems. In other words, behavioural experiments are done to counteract the client's presenting problems as seen in a hot-cross-bun formulation, for example.

Why Use Behavioural Experiments?

Personally, I would say why wouldn't you use them, but as great as thought records are because they allow the client to become more aware of their thinking and patterns of behaviour, and even come up with their own alternatives to these thoughts and behaviours. The person can still not be fully convinced that the alternatives are true.

As a result, behavioural experiments can:

- Test a client's unhelpful existing beliefs.
- Test out their new and more helpful beliefs
- Collect information to help develop the formulation further
- They enable experiential learning. Basically learning by doing.
- Allow clients to test out theory A versus Theory B

One of the ways and something that is very common in CBT is that a client will argue forever that they know what you're saying and the alternatives are true at a logical and fact level and they "feel it in my heart" and they "know it in their head" but they still refuse to believe it.

That's why behavioural experiments are very powerful ways to get them to see what happens when they drop their safety behaviours.

Of course, I'm not saying that behavioural experiments are easy for both the therapist and the client. Since the therapist needs to design behavioural experiments so, so carefully because if one of these experiments goes wrong then you have basically just confirmed outright a person's biased cognitive errors and beliefs. That isn't what you want.

Additionally, these can be difficult for the client because your therapist is basically making you confront something you absolutely hate.

However, if you ever see get a chance to see these experiments in practice as a student then definitely watch them. Since the one I watched was with an anxious woman who believed she would have sweat pouring off her, she would be violently shaking like an earthquake and she would be tomato red when she had to talk to a stranger so the therapist filmed an interaction and it turned out the woman was completely wrong.

She wasn't bright tomato red, she wasn't shaking (you really couldn't tell she was shaking at all) and no visual sweat was coming off her. This made the woman very surprised and happy and the therapist got the woman to do the experiment twice, once with safety behaviours and one without.

And you know what happened?

The woman admitted she looked so much more personable, likeable and human when she did the experiment without her safety behaviours.

It was a very powerful and fascinating thing to watch and enjoy.

On the whole, the purpose of behavioural

experiments is to get new information so the client can test the validity of their existing beliefs and cognitions. This includes them testing the content of these beliefs and cognitions and seeing the effect of their maladaptive processes. As well as behavioural experiments allow clients to create and test new, more adaptive beliefs and cognitions.

Finally, if we supply this information to anxiety disorders (the entire purpose of the book) then these experiments allow people to get new information to test the validity of the non-threatening explanation of anxiety and associated symptoms, and they help people to recognise that the anxiety-provoking situation they hate, isn't actually that dangerous in reality.

Behavioural Experiments: What Is Being Tested In Body Dysmorphia?

Bringing this back to body dysmorphia, the entire point of these experiments is to see the effects of the client engaging or not engaging in these safety behaviours. Then the client can see and test their preoccupation, strength of their beliefs and internal negative image, as well as their beliefs about negative evaluation and reactions from others.

A good behavioural experiment will show the client that their beliefs aren't correct and they don't reflect what is actually going on in the real world around them. This helps them to see that their fears aren't founded and they can use this new information to start changing their maladaptive coping mechanisms for healthier ones.

Equally, like I mentioned before, psychologists do need to be careful of directly testing a client's cognitions and beliefs, because they can be counterproductive and problematic. Especially if you accidentally confirm one of the biased Negative Automatic Thoughts in the process.

Something nobody wants at all.

EFFICACY OF CBT FOR BODY DYSMORPHIA, FUTURE RESEARCH AND MORE

To wrap up this section of the book before finishing off with the conclusion, because psychology is a science and clinical psychology is thankfully dedicated to the scientific method we need to look at the evidence saying whether CBT for Body Dysmorphia works or not.

Thankfully, there appears to be a lot of good evidence for the effectiveness and efficacy of CBT for Body Dysmorphia due to the UK's National Institute For Health and Care Excellent (NICE) recommends the use of CBT for Body Dysmorphia. For our international readers that is a big deal because NICE only ever recommends treatments that has the research to support it as a good treatment option.

In addition, there are studies showing the effectiveness of CBT for Body Dysmorphia in adults. For example, Rosen et al. (1995); Veale et al (1996);

McKay (1997); Wilhelm et al. (2014); Rabiei et al. (2012); Veale et al (2014); Veale et al (follow-up) (2015); Enander et al. (2016).

I know that was a lot of citations but one interesting thing in that list is the years. Since these show that CBT for Body Dysmorphia has always been effective and it is good that research has continued to not only show this effectiveness, but we're starting to look at other facets of CBT too.

More on that later.

Furthermore, there is a good amount of research that CBT for Body Dysmorphia works well for adolescents as well. such as, Mataix-Cols et al. (2015); Greenberg et al. (2016); Krebs et al. (follow-up) (2017).

Again, I think after the hard topics looked at in this book, I definitely think these are good findings and very encouraging for the future. Due to yes, eating disorders and Body Dysmorphia is very hard to treat, yes the conditions kill people and success rate is very low compared to other psychotherapies for other mental health conditions.

But there is hope.

Also, one major, major point that is a strong advantage of CBT for Body Dysmorphia is that the research uses Meta-analyses and systemic reviews of Randomized Controlled Trials (RCTs). If you've the bonus essay at the back of CBT for Depression then you'll be familiar why this is such great news.

However, RCTs are the gold standard of research and they are the only way to truly tell, according to Bhide et al. (2018), if a cause and effect relationship exists. For example, if CBT for Body Dysmorphia leads to a reduction in symptoms or if there is another factor involved causing the decrease.

Therefore, the fact that the CBT for Body Dysmorphia uses their research methodology only strengthens the evidence supporting it. these reviews include Prazeres et al. (2012), Harrison et al. (2016) and Phillipou et al. (2016).

RCT CBT vs Anxiety Management

Furthermore, to show the effectiveness of CBT, I wanted to show you the results of Veale et al. (2014) because it is a great study to look at.

As a result of the participants were randomised to either 12 weekly sessions of CBT or Anxiety Management treatment and the sample was stratified for delusional disorder and severity of depression. Also, the main outcome measurement was the Yale-Brown Obsessive-Compulsive Scale Modified for Body Dysmorphic Disorder (BDD-YBOCS) done by a blind observer.

Then both groups did a baseline and the measurements were taken again at week 6 and week 12. As well as the CBT went on for 16 weeks, 6 months or 1 year.

As a result, the study found that rather unsurprisingly Cognitive Behavioural Therapy was found to be significantly better than Anxiety

Management at Week 12 on the BDD-YBOCS as well as the secondary outcome measures of the Assessment of Beliefs Scale, Appearance Anxiety Inventory and Body Image Quality of Life Inventory.

Nonetheless, even though the study still showed that CBT is a good treatment option, the condition is still very hard to treat with 15% of the participants showing no improvement and 56% showing only partial remission.

Of course, the benefit of the study was that it used anxiety management as the control so at least it was an active comparator and not a passive one.

However, there were real problems with the study because it was a small sample size. Therefore, the study recommended developing new treatment modules to help the clients recover more and optimize the length of therapy to 24 sessions and maintenance follow ups.

The problem with the last recommendation though is 24 sessions (6 months) is that is a lot of money to spend for public sector mental health services, so I doubt it would ever happen until government budgets increase dramatically which they won't.

Source: Veale, D., Anson, M., Miles, S., Pieta, M., Costa, A., & Ellison, N. (2014). Efficacy of cognitive behaviour therapy versus anxiety management for body dysmorphic disorder, A randomised controlled trial. Psychotherapy & Psychosomatics, 83, 341-353.

Future research For Body Dysmorphia

In the future, when it comes to researching body dysmorphia, there is a lot to do to be honest, because we ideally need a treatment that works for the majority of people. As well as we need RCTs to be used when comparing CBT to placebos and (for some reason I don't know why some researchers mention this avenue) Selective Serotonin Reuptake Inhibitors.

Then hopefully when we know for sure that CBT is the best psychological treatment option then we need to find out why. And this is part of a research movement that I'm very excited about because researchers want to unbundle CBT to find out what modules of the therapy are the most important. Then the theory is only when we know what modules are the most important, we can put them together to create a super-CBT for something.

And that seriously is what we need for eating disorders and Body Dysmorphia.

Finally, when it comes to future research, we need to determine the best length of treatment, not only for Body Dysmorphia itself, but for comorbidity too, because clients might need to continue to 20-30 sessions, but we need a bit of research for that fact.

After all that I definitely think if you want a real challenging area of clinical psychology to research then certainly consider researching Body Dysmorphia.

It will keep you busy that's for sure.

Support For Body Dysmorphia

Just to wrap up this final chapter, I have to admit that I simply don't know why you, wonderful reader, picked up this book. You might be a psychology student or mental health professional wanting to learn more, you might be a layperson wondering what the hell CBT is, or you might be someone concerned about a friend or love one who you suspect might have Body Dysmorphia or an eating disorder.

Nothing in this book is any sort of official advice, but if you, yourself, or someone you know or love needs support then you might want to check out these resources.

There's always therapy and support groups available if you look around for them. In the UK, there is the charity, OCD Action www.ocdaction.org.uk or www.bddfoundation.org and I know that other countries have similar things.

But please, if you need professional help do get it.

CONCLUSION

Even though this is now my third psychology book that focuses on Cognitive Behavioural Therapy, I have to say that I still love the topic, because if you've read the other two books on Anxiety and Depression then you know what I mean when I say that each one is different.

Since the great thing about CBT is that it is so structural and it gives you a brilliant manualised way to treat mental health conditions by challenging their cognitions through the process of behavioural activation and cognitive restructuring.

Then that simple base or foundation gives you a lot of freedom to apply the theories and cognitive interventions to a wide range of mental health conditions, and of course CBT isn't perfect (it seriously isn't) but it still gives us a lot of great tools and techniques to use with clients.

That's why I really recommend you read CBT For Depression and CBT For Anxiety as well, because each book shows you different things about CBT. For example, this book I've just read focuses slightly on the theory side and really explores the different eating disorders and body dysmorphia more. I did that because there is a lot to cover.

I did a similar thing in CBT For Anxiety because there are a lot of anxiety disorders to understand and each one of them uses CBT slightly differently.

Whereas for CBT For Depression, I focused a lot more on the CBT side and I explored the therapy side of the book in a lot, lot more depth.

None of these books are necessarily better than the other and I had a blast writing all of them, but my point is that CBT is very flexible if you know how to apply it to different mental health conditions, as well as CBT gives us a lot of techniques and tools we can use with different therapeutic models too.

Therefore, I really hope you found this book useful and now you understand what eating disorders are and how they're treated. I really enjoyed writing it, exploring these topics and hopefully offering some hope along the way.

I know that eating disorders and body dysmorphia and how deadly they are, can make them dark topics. Yet research is always happening, CBT is still the most effective option we have and it is being delivered by bright, passionate and amazing therapists all over the world.

So there is always hope and I truly believe that in

the future as more research happens and our understanding grows, that one day having an eating disorder will no longer be a death sentence.

That is a future I would love to live in and I am really looking forward to when that day comes.

https://www.subscribepage.com/psychologyboxset

CHECK OUT THE PSYCHOLOGY WORLD PODCAST FOR MORE PSYCHOLOGY INFORMATION! AVAILABLE ON ALL MAJOR PODCAST APPS.

About the author:

Connor Whiteley is the author of over 60 books in the sci-fi fantasy, nonfiction psychology and books for writer's genre and he is a Human Branding Speaker and Consultant.

He is a passionate warhammer 40,000 reader, psychology student and author.

Who narrates his own audiobooks and he hosts The Psychology World Podcast.

All whilst studying Psychology at the University of Kent, England.

Also, he was a former Explorer Scout where he gave a speech to the Maltese President in August 2018 and he attended Prince Charles' 70th Birthday Party at Buckingham Palace in May 2018.

Plus, he is a self-confessed coffee lover!

CBT FOR EATING DISORDERS AND BODY DYSMORPHIC DISORDER

<u>Other books by Connor Whiteley:</u>
<u>All books in 'An Introductory Series':</u>
Careers In Psychology
Psychology of Suicide
Dementia Psychology
Clinical Psychology Reflections Volume 4
Forensic Psychology of Terrorism And Hostage-Taking
Forensic Psychology of False Allegations
Year In Psychology
CBT For Anxiety
CBT For Depression
Applied Psychology
<u>BIOLOGICAL PSYCHOLOGY 3RD EDITION</u>
<u>COGNITIVE PSYCHOLOGY THIRD EDITION</u>
<u>SOCIAL PSYCHOLOGY- 3RD EDITION</u>
<u>ABNORMAL PSYCHOLOGY 3RD EDITION</u>
<u>PSYCHOLOGY OF RELATIONSHIPS- 3RD EDITION</u>
<u>DEVELOPMENTAL PSYCHOLOGY 3RD EDITION</u>
<u>HEALTH PSYCHOLOGY</u>
<u>RESEARCH IN PSYCHOLOGY</u>
<u>A GUIDE TO MENTAL HEALTH AND</u>

TREATMENT AROUND THE WORLD- A GLOBAL LOOK AT DEPRESSION
FORENSIC PSYCHOLOGY
THE FORENSIC PSYCHOLOGY OF THEFT, BURGLARY AND OTHER CRIMES AGAINST PROPERTY
CRIMINAL PROFILING: A FORENSIC PSYCHOLOGY GUIDE TO FBI PROFILING AND GEOGRAPHICAL AND STATISTICAL PROFILING.
CLINICAL PSYCHOLOGY
FORMULATION IN PSYCHOTHERAPY
PERSONALITY PSYCHOLOGY AND INDIVIDUAL DIFFERENCES
CLINICAL PSYCHOLOGY REFLECTIONS VOLUME 1
CLINICAL PSYCHOLOGY REFLECTIONS VOLUME 2
Clinical Psychology Reflections Volume 3
CULT PSYCHOLOGY
Police Psychology

A Psychology Student's Guide To University
How Does University Work?
A Student's Guide To University And Learning
University Mental Health and Mindset

Bettie English Private Eye Series
A Very Private Woman
The Russian Case
A Very Urgent Matter
A Case Most Personal
Trains, Scots and Private Eyes
The Federation Protects
Cops, Robbers and Private Eyes
Just Ask Bettie English
An Inheritance To Die For
The Death of Graham Adams
Bearing Witness
The Twelve
The Wrong Body
The Assassination Of Bettie English

Lord of War Origin Trilogy:
Not Scared Of The Dark
Madness
Burn Them All

The Fireheart Fantasy Series
Heart of Fire
Heart of Lies
Heart of Prophecy
Heart of Bones
Heart of Fate

City of Assassins (Urban Fantasy)
City of Death
City of Marytrs
City of Pleasure
City of Power

Agents of The Emperor
Return of The Ancient Ones
Vigilance
Angels of Fire
Kingmaker
The Eight
The Lost Generation
Hunt
Emperor's Council
Speaker of Treachery
Birth Of The Empire
Terraforma

The Rising Augusta Fantasy Adventure Series
Rise To Power
Rising Walls
Rising Force
Rising Realm

<u>Lord Of War Trilogy (Agents of The Emperor)</u>
Not Scared Of The Dark
Madness
Burn It All Down

<u>Gay Romance Novellas</u>
Breaking, Nursing, Repairing A Broken Heart
Jacob And Daniel
Fallen For A Lie
Spying And Weddings

<u>Miscellaneous:</u>
RETURN
FREEDOM
SALVATION
Reflection of Mount Flame
The Masked One
The Great Deer
English Independence

OTHER SHORT STORIES BY CONNOR WHITELEY

<u>Mystery Short Story Collections</u>
Criminally Good Stories Volume 1: 20 Detective Mystery Short Stories
Criminally Good Stories Volume 2: 20 Private Investigator Short Stories
Criminally Good Stories Volume 3: 20 Crime Fiction Short Stories
Criminally Good Stories Volume 4: 20 Science Fiction and Fantasy Mystery Short Stories
Criminally Good Stories Volume 5: 20 Romantic Suspense Short Stories

<u>Mystery Short Stories:</u>
Protecting The Woman She Hated
Finding A Royal Friend
Our Woman In Paris
Corrupt Driving
A Prime Assassination
Jubilee Thief
Jubilee, Terror, Celebrations
Negative Jubilation
Ghostly Jubilation
Killing For Womenkind
A Snowy Death

CBT FOR EATING DISORDERS AND BODY DYSMORPHIC DISORDER

Miracle Of Death
A Spy In Rome
The 12:30 To St Pancreas
A Country In Trouble
A Smokey Way To Go
A Spicy Way To GO
A Marketing Way To Go
A Missing Way To Go
A Showering Way To Go
Poison In The Candy Cane
Kendra Detective Mystery Collection Volume 1
Kendra Detective Mystery Collection Volume 2
Mystery Short Story Collection Volume 1
Mystery Short Story Collection Volume 2
Criminal Performance
Candy Detectives
Key To Birth In The Past

<u>Science Fiction Short Stories:</u>
Their Brave New World
Gummy Bear Detective
The Candy Detective
What Candies Fear
The Blurred Image
Shattered Legions

The First Rememberer
Life of A Rememberer
System of Wonder
Lifesaver
Remarkable Way She Died
The Interrogation of Annabella Stormic
Blade of The Emperor
Arbiter's Truth
Computation of Battle
Old One's Wrath
Puppets and Masters
Ship of Plague
Interrogation
Edge of Failure

Fantasy Short Stories:
City of Snow
City of Light
City of Vengeance
Dragons, Goats and Kingdom
Smog The Pathetic Dragon
Don't Go In The Shed
The Tomato Saver
The Remarkable Way She Died
Dragon Coins
Dragon Tea
Dragon Rider

www.ingramcontent.com/pod-product-compliance
Lightning Source LLC
LaVergne TN
LVHW011828060526
838200LV00053B/3934